the five core
conversations
for
couples

Expert Advice about How to Develop:

- Effective Communication
- A Long-Term Financial Plan
- Cooperative Parenting Strategies
- Mutually Satisfying Sex
- Work-Life Balance

DAVID BULITT, JD
divorce and family lawyer

JULIE BULITT, LCSW-C
family therapist

Skyhorse Publishing

Skyhorse Publishing books may be purchased in bulk at special discounts for sales promotion, corporate gifts, fund-raising, or educational purposes. Special editions can also be created to specifications. For details, contact the Special Sales Department, Skyhorse Publishing, 307 West 36th Street, 11th Floor, New York, NY 10018 or info@skyhorsepublishing.com.

Skyhorse® and Skyhorse Publishing® are registered trademarks of Skyhorse Publishing, Inc.®, a Delaware corporation.

Visit our website at www.skyhorsepublishing.com.

10 9 8 7 6 5 4 3 2 1

Library of Congress Cataloging-in-Publication Data is available on file.

Cover design by Daniel Brount
Cover illustrations by gettyimages

Print ISBN: 978-1-5107-4612-1
Ebook ISBN: 978-1-5107-4613-8

Table of Contents

Introduction: Who Are We? Why Are We Here? vii

The First Core: Building and Filling 1

1. Connection is Your Lubrication 5
2. The Garage Will Get Dirty 8
3. Fix the Roof 11
4. Use Your Oxygen Mask 14
5. The RV 17
6. I Don't Give a Shit about the Dry Cleaning 20
7. Silence Is Not Golden 24
8. It's Not What You Say, It's How You Say It 27
9. If It Won't Matter, Don't Say It 31
10. I Think I Can, I Know We Can 35
 Couple's Kickstarters 38

The Second Core: Money, Money, Money 41

1. Fun, Fun, Fun till Reality Takes Your T-Bird Away 43
2. You Canceled My Newspaper? 46
3. Learn to Drive before You're Sixty-Five 50
4. A Balance of Power 53
5. Don't Wait for the Repo Man 56
6. Don't Bank the Bitching 60
7. Harvard 63
8. Cash and Kids 66

9. The Swimming Pool   69
Couple's Kickstarters   72

The Third Core: Parents and Partners   75

1. The Adoption Option   78
2. Pass the Trash   82
3. Voted off the Island   85
4. Make It, Take It   88
5. Jesus Joins the Family   91
6. No One Sends You Dinner When Your Kid Is
   in the Psych Ward   95
7. Sticks and Stones   98
8. Addiction Finds Us   101
9. Ride in the Same Ambulance   104
10. Letters to Our Daughter   109
11. To Our Other Three   114
Couple's Kickstarters   116

The Fourth Core: Bumping and Grinding   119

1. It's Not a Budget Item   122
2. Tussies   125
3. That's Not My Finger   128
4. Is That All There Is?   131
5. A Hitch in Your Giddyup   134
6. To Porn or Not to Porn   138
7. Is There Even Such a Thing?   142
8. I Don't Need Another Job   145
9. Two Minutes and a Tissue   148
Couple's Kickstarters   151

The Fifth Core: It's a Balancing Act   155

1. Costco   158
2. Cussing to Kissing   161
3. Assbook   164

4. More or Less   167
5. The Minivan   171
6. Bumper Cars   174
7. Stay out of My Tub   177
8. You've Got to Have Friends   180
9. Weekends Away   183
10. Ruby Slippers   186
11. The Best Chicken in the Pot I Ever Ate   189
Couple's Kickstarters   192

The Takeaway: On and On   197
About the Authors   199
Acknowledgments   201
Index   202

Who Are We? Why Are We Here?

I have a lover's spat and a few drinks to thank for thirty-plus years with my wife. It was an early spring Saturday night at a fraternity party just off-campus from the University of Maryland. Julie was eighteen, angry with her freshman-year boyfriend, and out to have a few beers. I was three years older, ready to graduate and start law school. Roaming with my buddies, my goal was simple: I was looking to get laid. Having compared our own versions of that night a few dozen times over the years, I think she saw me first. Her portrayal is a bit more love at first sight; mine tilts toward simple lust. But we spent hours together, at the party and after. I planned to play it cool and wait a few days to call, until I broke down and phoned her the next afternoon. We have been pinned together ever since.

Julie is probably the most well-rounded person I have ever met. No, she can't sing, but she can manage, work and think her way through most anything that our day-to-day lives throw her way. She is empathetic (with everyone but me anyway), always happy to help a neighbor or friend with a dinner when someone is sick, or a free therapy session even when it's the cousin of a friend's friend who needs to talk. Julie will stop, chat, and engage with anyone. She's the girl that once you have decided to leave the party, it takes her another hour or so to say goodbye because she stops and talks to nine people on her way out.

A good friend of ours once said to me, "I can never get me enough Julie Bulitt." I feel the same. Smart, insightful, great looking, and reliably hilarious, Julie was a good catch. That is not to say that she is without her transgressions—she can fart and snore like nobody's business, has a knack for getting into interpersonal conflicts with strangers, and isn't exactly the most affectionate character in the world. Nevertheless, how it was that she, a family therapist, ended up with me, an often jaded, overly pessimistic, and habitually unsociable divorce lawyer is quite the curiosity.

Julie would probably tell you that I have many redeeming qualities. A running joke between us is that she married me because I "know how to go places." To someone who gets lost with regularity, I suppose that having a partner that "knows how to go places" is a good thing, albeit a little less useful with the advent of Google Maps and Waze. Julie likes that I am dependable. Like a good sense of direction, dependability is not a quality that stirs a Brad Pitt sort of sexiness for a lot of women, but being someone Julie can count on has certainly helped push me into the black, so to speak. I am a decent storyteller, helped by my ability to improve my exaggeration with each retelling. Patience? Don't have too much of that except with my kids, grandchildren, and dogs, but Julie doesn't seem to mind telling me to "press my P button" when I need to. I will also tell you that I am a pro at saying I am sorry, something that has no doubt developed from having had to do so with abundance and regularity.

When couples marry, they often repeat the traditional marriage vows. Both partners promise to have and hold the other, from that day forward, for better or for worse, in sickness and in health, until death do they part. For many of us, that can be a tough row to hoe. When the eighties rock singer Meat Loaf topped off a famous tune with the lyric "I'm praying for the end of time, so I can end my time with you," trust me, he wasn't the only one.

During the course of our marriage, Julie and I have had the usual share of conversations and colloquies, debates and disputes. More than thirty years of talking. Talking about our relationship and other couples and their relationships, about our problems and their problems, our kids and their kids, money that we wish we had, money we shouldn't have spent, not having enough sex, being harassed into too much sex. Several years ago, though, it struck me that our decades-long and still running marital reel-to-reel might be different in some way—unique, possibly—than other couples. While we are a couple, we are also in the business of relationships, saving them and ending them. What do a divorce lawyer and a family therapist talk about when the doors are closed, when the alcohol is flowing, when they are in the bathtub or walking on the beach? What's on our minds? What makes us laugh, yell, and cry? Who gets the last word?

From our differing vantage points and often contrasting perspectives, Julie and I have seen up close families struggling with life's most difficult challenges, including infidelity, mental health diagnoses, learning disabilities, abuse, serious illness, estrangement, and trauma. At the same time, we have weathered our own challenges at home, raised four daughters, two biological and two adopted, and dealt with one child's mental health and behavioral issues, addiction, running away, and pregnancy.

What we have listened to, struggled through, and learned about saving a marriage, keeping a family together, or knowing when to call it quits, when to turn to professionals, or when to try tough love, could fill a book. And it has. This book is culled from my notes and memories of our many discussions, disagreements, and more than a few arguments. Sectioned topically into the five core building blocks to all successful relationships, our conversations include funny, frank, and sometimes painful stories and issues. We go back and forth and tackle the basics from getting along, to parenting, communication, finances, and sex, as well as hard-to-discuss issues like addiction, infertility, pornography, adultery, and family silence.

Here is, for better or for worse, what we talk about. We hope it helps you to gain some fresh insights into your own relationships and have valuable and more frequent conversations with those you love.

—*David*

THE FIRST CORE
Building and Filling

I see a lot of people in my practice that struggle with relationships. They have a hard time getting along at work, have conflicts with their parents and children, and aren't happy with their partner. The adage "build it and they will come" is partially true, particularly when it comes to a relationship. Like any structure designed to last, a solid relationship requires some basic building blocks. Just as you can't have one layer of brick followed by another layer of vinyl siding, two people have to share a common material view of their lives together: Do we have similar likes and dislikes? Do we complement each other? Are our values aligned? And what about children? Do we both want to have them? Do we generally agree on spending versus saving? How much does sex matter and how much is enough? How do we fight? Can this person balance life's challenges and work, but still be there for me when I need them?

Unfortunately, there isn't one simple rubric of questions to ask before embarking on a committed relationship. There are general questions you can ask, but each couple needs to also figure out his or particular deal breakers, whether it's money, sex, kids, or in-laws. What I can tell you, though, is that people who are able to stay together, weather life's storms and struggles together (and that is the important word here, *together*), those people have built that foundation. They understand where they are aligned, and work to improve the areas where they aren't.

The work doesn't end once you have poured the concrete and put up the pillars. Building your relationship infrastructure doesn't answer the question: The foundation is sound, but will the two of you stay grounded? When your building first opened, it was spectacular and beautiful; it seemed solid. The ribbon cutting was a success, people came and raised their glasses and offered up toasts to the lovely couple. But what if the floors aren't kept clean? The plumbing and air conditioning aren't serviced? Filters aren't changed, leaks aren't fixed, and walls aren't repainted? We all know the answer; the structure starts to fail and break down. Years later the shine is off and in many cases the building begins to tear down, leaving nothing but a remnant of the past.

Many couples have come to me over the years, their relationship in a similar state of disrepair. One or both partners feel isolated, underappreciated, and often lonely. They have not spent the time needed to keep their relationship intact, and as a result, it has become unfulfilling and empty.

Sarah and Ron were in my office late in the afternoon on a Wednesday. They were stiff and our greetings were forced; stress seeped from their pores. Sarah sat down first; Ron dropped into the chair farthest away. Married for seven years with two small children at home, Sarah also worked full time. We talked a lot about her feeling burdened with the not uncommon stresses of work and being a parent. She was overwhelmed.

"By the time I get the kids at five, we aren't home until close to six and then it's a rush to get dinner made, baths done, laundry moving. I don't have any time to play or read or laugh. I can't enjoy being a mom because I am so hurried all the time," she told me.

I suggested to Sarah that she try to get out of the office earlier a day or two a week, which would enable her to get her children from daycare on time, and have a schedule that would allow her to do at least some of the things that she wanted and felt were missing.

"And when was the last time you spent time together, just the two of you?" I asked them. "No kids, no work, no laundry or cleaning?"

Sarah was blank; she stared at me as if I had asked the question in a foreign language. After a long pause, she realized it had been over a year. "We don't talk that much about it, to tell you the truth. We both work, he's out of the house before me and the kids are up, and by the time the kids are in bed, that's where I want to be. In bed and asleep, before we start right up again the next day," she said.

"I think it was back in 2015," Ron told me as he rolled his eyes. "We watched the last episode of *Mad Men*."

As a result of no "adult alone time" Sarah and Ron were spending their first alone time with me. I told them to go to the candy store. Sarah laughed. Ron's eyes bulged and his black glasses slid down over his nose.

I explained that when I was little my mom would take me to a clothing store called the Acorn Shop in Canton, Massachusetts, near where I grew up. I was always excited to go with her to the store not because I liked shopping for clothes. (At seven or eight years old, what kid likes shopping for clothes?) And the Acorn Shop was a women's clothing store—nothing at all for kids. But when my mom brought me to the store, the owner, Irving, immediately gave me fifty cents and sent me to the candy shop a few doors down. I was happy for at least an hour and that gave my mom time to try on clothes. With fifty cents, I could afford to stuff my bag with Fireballs, Pixy Stix, Wax Lips, Candy Cigarettes and more. I was literally the kid in the candy store. Adults need candy shops; adults in relationships need time in the candy shop both alone and together.

"This is the kind of time you two want to spend together," I told them. "Not every day, obviously, but with some regularity. Give your-self something to look forward to, and then focus on each other. It can be anything. A walk in the neighborhood, watching TV together, going out for a quick dinner. Adults need candy shops, too!"

Back in my office a couple of weeks later, Sarah and Ron were more at ease. They held hands on the way in and sat closer together. I asked about the candy store. Sarah said it went well. They got a neighborhood teen to babysit and made plans to get home early from work on a weeknight. "Something that never happens," Sarah said. In the grand scheme of life, it wasn't a huge event. The two of them just had some wine and a couple of appetizers at a nearby restaurant and after a couple of hours came home to a quiet house.

"We had our phones in case the kids needed us, but no Facebook, checking email, or texting. It was just the two of us and since it was a Wednesday the place was fairly quiet. It was like we had the whole place to ourselves," Ron said.

"It was lovely," Sarah added.

More trips to the candy store were planned, Sarah told me. Ron responded with an enthusiastic "thumbs up."

I don't mean to suggest that a trip to the candy store now and again will keep every relationship on course. If that were the case, I would be rich and David would be out of business, but a healthy relationship requires not only that it be built from the ground up, so to speak, but also that it be tended to, nurtured, and filled. And you can't wait too long to do it—if you do, you run the risk of having nothing to say.

–Julie

Connection is Your Lubrication

"You can't just feel a connection; you have to make a connection and strive to maintain it. Like a personal trainer says: work, grind, eat, sleep, and then repeat."

–Julie

The term "connection" is overused. Just watch an episode of *The Bachelor* and you will probably hear some reference to the "connection" that multiple strangers have made, are making, or are going to make at least a dozen times during the hour-long program. The concept of making a connection is soaked into our relationship blanket. The word itself is thrown and tossed around—and not just on TV—without much thought about what it means to make a connection, and what it really represents in terms of developing and maintaining a relationship. The connection that you have with your partner is what helps it stick. When it's there, it works. When it isn't, things start to fail.

When I mention connection as a relationship's lubrication, David's knee-jerk response is along the lines of "tell me more about the lubrication." A one-trick pony now and again, my husband is. Of course, sex has something to do with your relationship being strong, you being "connected" to your partner. I tell people to look at a relationship like a car's engine. Most engines need oil (or lubrication) to run. No oil, the engine overheats, breaks down. It's the same thing in a relationship. No lubrication and the relationship falters and stalls. It dies out.

"So, where does the lubrication come in?" David asks.

I tell clients, and my husband, that lubrication is what maintains that connection between two people. The point is that it's not some word on a reality show, it is meaningful, and complex, and can take many forms. It can be that cup of coffee together in the morning, a cocktail at night. Taking a walk, talking about what went on at work during the day. It can be sharing the highs, the lows of being a parent. Getting dressed and going out on a date. Working together, respecting each other. All of that.

If it seems pretty basic, that's because it is. Sometimes people build connections in other, more unexpected kinds of ways. Many couples connect through their children. One partner might feel more of a kind of closeness, or feel a different appreciation when the other is just doing something simple with their child. It could be as simple as reading a book or giving the child a bath.

"What about changing a diaper?" David asks. Sure. Even changing a diaper. You know, it's something like, "Hey, I fell for this guy at school, at a bar, wherever. But now look at him, taking care of my baby." In that situation, it's warmth, a different type of feeling that keeps things lubricated.

And of course, the opposite is true as well. If one partner doesn't do their share with that child, does not want to read, give her a bath, the other might feel angry. Or disappointed. And neither is good. Both of those feelings are harmful to the couple's connection, particularly if they persist.

So, what happens when there has been a lengthy period between two people when things have not been good? They have not gotten along for whatever the reason. Are they destined to head to my husband's office? Although not helpful to David's divorce practice, my own experience is no. All of us go through ebbs and flows in relationships. The key to getting through the "ebbs," is to work harder on the "flows."

At our house, nothing works better to keep me aware and appreciative of him than when David vacuums, cleans the house, takes out the trash, that sort of thing. Those are important to me. He knows they are. So, if we are in a down time or a period where neither of us is feeling great about the other, and I notice he is working hard at doing things that make me happy and matter to me, how does that make me feel? You know the answer. I feel better about us. Closer again.

In my practice, I regularly remind people that relationships are not perfect; everything is not seamless all of the time. If you love your partner, then you need to work to pull the two of you out of those periods. Sometimes it can be as easy as just telling someone how you feel or a small little gesture like a hug or holding his hand.

I don't mean to make it sound like it's all that simple. If every relationship could be fixed, re-lubricated as I call it, with an "I love you" or a quick peck on the cheek, David would be looking for work. To be honest, we both might be out of work. But no, that is not what I mean. I am not suggesting that an act of kindness, or a few nice words are going to magically fix everything. It's a strategy to help. Not every strategy works for everyone or in every instance.

Let me get to my husband's priority question number one. What about sex? Can that provide lubrication in a relationship? Of course it can. Sex is part of that connection. It is often a big part. If a couple has sex regularly, they can feel more connected, happier, and more comfortable in their relationship. It's not the only thing, but it is definitely important, in most relationships anyway.

If people feel connected, they can get over the small stuff, like when David pees on the toilet seat or shaves and leaves the hair clippings in the bathroom for me to wipe off the sink, or when I leave the lights on, turn the heat up to seventy-five degrees at the first day under seventy in the fall, and keep talking about the same thing multiple times over several days. If there wasn't that connection, that intimacy, that closeness, those kinds of things gum up the relationship and break it down. Just like cars.

The Garage Will Get Dirty

"Why you can't let stuff slide, big stuff or little stuff."

—*David*

One job I really hate is cleaning the garage. Every spring, it's just misery. No matter how much time I spent sweeping, hosing, and purging just a year earlier, I still get that, "It's about that time again," from Julie.

It's the same script every year.

Me: "And what time would that be?"

Julie: "It's getting warmer, the garage is a mess."

Me: "The garage is always a mess."

Julie: "Not after you clean it."

Me: "That is an awful job."

Julie: "It's not that bad."

Me: "I just cleaned it."

Julie: "That was a year ago."

Me: "It doesn't seem that long."

On top of it, after spending four or five hours on a Saturday throwing shit out that accumulated since last year, wiping down the shelves, and organizing all the rest, inevitably when the kids take toys and bikes out and don't put them back, trash piles up, dogs track in dirt, and the wind blows leaves in, it just gets dirty again. Seems like such a waste. In reality, though, it isn't a waste. Why should I think that the garage is any different from the rest of the house? That it should stay clean because I cleaned it? We clean our house most every day in some way. Counters get wiped down, a rug gets vacuumed, shelves and tables cleaned and dusted. "And if you think about it, cleaning the garage is just what people need to do to keep a relationship healthy," Julie tells me.

I have a difficult time with the "clean garage, healthy relationship" metaphor. What exactly is the metaphor queen telling me? That sweeping the other person aside and into the trash keeps the relationship going strong? "It's a mistake that some people make in their relationships," Julie says. "They date, fall in love, and maybe get married. They are committed to each other. But they let things slide."

Grudgingly, I have to admit that it makes sense. People who have been together for years don't take care of themselves. How they dress, how they look. I see it all the time in my office. The person you got involved with a few years ago doesn't look like she used to, she doesn't take care of herself like she used to. But there is more to it than letting oneself down physically. It's paying attention to what the other has to say, put the paper down when your partner is talking, don't check your phone during dinner. People need to continuously be working on keeping the relationship happy and healthy. And what happens if they don't? Better be ready to spend several hundred dollars of your hard-earned money on someone like me sitting on the other side of a desk so that a stranger in a black robe can make decisions about the future of your family.

Remember the garage. Keeping the garage clean takes work. And not just every spring. Every day. If there is something on the floor, pick it up. Don't wait an hour or a week or six months to do it. If the garage needs a quick sweep, then sweep it. A healthy relationship needs the same sort of attention.

I don't profess to be a therapist or even the slightest bit creative when it comes to thinking up metaphors like my wife can. But this idea is simple, even for me. Your relationship garage gets cleaned and swept by spending time with your partner, doing nice things for him, talking to her, and at least now and then, having sex with each other.

So, what are you waiting for? Go get your broom.

Fix the Roof

"If you wouldn't let the roof on your house rot and cave in, why wouldn't you put the same attention into the relationship living under that roof?"

—*David*

From the garage, let's move to the roof. My wife has an analogy, a loopy connection between relationships and, it appears, just about every room, wall, and appliance in the house. And fixing a roof? That has to be worse than buying new tires for your car. Both cost too much and, to make it even worse, who the hell even notices?

"We have been in this house for twenty years. You have to take care of the roof," she says.

This time it is leaking over my daughter's window. A couple of months ago we needed shingles replaced. Never ending.

Julie looks at me and shoots me her I-had-a-brilliant-thought look. "Yes?"

"That is interesting," she says.

"What exactly is interesting about it? I am talking about having to sink more money into this house to keep the roof from caving in and you think it is interesting? Plus, I already know what's coming," I say.

The relationship metaphor.

"This exact thing came up in one of my sessions today," Julie says.

I think maybe I need to pour me a short glass of bourbon.

"It won't take too long," she promises. "You know how people say they don't have time to do things they want to do?"

"Of course I do. People complain about that all the time. Friends, family, everyone. It's a regular occurrence when people are in my office talking about divorce."

"That's where I am going," she says. "People are so busy that there is no time for exercise, to read, sit, or just talk to their partner. It can be anything. We can't take the time to do what we want to do or what we need to do."

"Sometimes they are the same thing," I say.

"That is true."

It seems I am on the right path so I keep at it. "I might *want* to go where it is quiet and listen to some music, but in some ways, it is something I *need* to do. Same with going out and seeing my friends."

"And you look forward to those things," Julie says. "The music helps you relax; you get enjoyment out of it. And spending time with your friends serves a similar purpose. It is fun, sure, but it is also good for you. You get out, away from the everyday stuff at home, laugh, and talk with your buddies."

"You don't want to know what we talk about," I remind her.

"I try not to think about it," she says. "Anyway, this woman, Gail, comes to see me today. She is not only unhappy with her husband, Jeff, but just miserable with her life in general."

"And this somehow has to do with our spending more of our savings patching holes in the roof?" I ask.

"Yes. Her hair was dirty, pulled back in a scruffy ponytail. She is so stuck worrying about her day-to-day tasks, that she does not take the time needed to keep herself together, much less take the time to keep relationship house in order. Gail spent much of our first forty or so minutes together just moping and complaining. Woe is me, my life stinks, I don't have any fun, I work, take care of my kids, I eat and I sleep."

"So, what did you suggest to sad Gail?"

"I told her that those tasks would always be there. She needs to make the time to focus on what is good for her, what is good for her relationship with Jeff," responds Julie Bulitt, Executive Functioning Coach. "Like a lot of people, Gail has shitty time management skills. She puts off the important stuff until it is too late."

"It's like the leaky roof is what you are saying," I say, adding no insight whatsoever into the conversation. This is a typical discussion for us when it comes to a lot of things—Julie leads, I follow.

"Yes, like the leaky roof. When you have a roof that leaks, you need to fix it. You don't wait, let it go, or worry about it later. You need to find the time to deal with it now, right?" she asks, already knowing the answer.

"Sure, we would call a roofer and put a bucket down in the meantime. One of us would stay home from work, rearrange our schedule, and do whatever we need to do to make sure the leak gets fixed," I say.

"Because?"

"Because it will get worse if we don't. The roof might cave in," I respond.

"Right. We would find the time to get it fixed. It's the same thing for Gail. She needs to stop ignoring those things that she needs to do for herself and in her relationship with Jeff. She wouldn't stand around and let water leak in and wreck her house," Julie says, bringing the two ends closer together.

"She would find the time to fix it," I say.

"Of course. Like the water that will inevitably damage the house, failing to find the time to tend to yourself and your relationship with your partner will do the same thing."

"Sounds like it could get messy."

"It will," Julie answers.

Relationships that get messy? That's why I stay in business.

Use Your Oxygen Mask

"Everybody needs a breath now and again."

–Julie

Do you ever pay attention when the flight attendant on a plane shows you how to use those oxygen masks? Of course you don't. No one does. After all, it doesn't seem like rocket science, to be honest. The things drop down; you put them over your head and face and start breathing. Of course, you do have to remember that if something goes awry when you are traveling with kids, your mask goes on first, the child's after. Why wouldn't you first help your daughter to make sure she can breathe, and then take care of yourself? As parents, we all generally put our kids' safety before ours, don't we? I should put my mask on before my kid's? It's not right, is it?

But here's the thing. It is. On a plane, you can't help your child if you are suffocating. Make sure you can breathe first, and then move on to others who need your help. It is the same with being a partner, a spouse, or a parent. I tell clients that an oxygen mask isn't what you need to be a parent, it's what you need to be a *good* parent, an effective parent. While this may seem a little counterintuitive, there is nothing particularly creative or new about this concept. Think about it for a moment. Do you do your best work at the office when you are rested and healthy or tired and feeling bad?

Of course, we are all more effective at our jobs when our minds are clear, when we are feeling fresh and sharp. When my kids were little, I was home all day, day in, day out. David went off to work, came home eight or ten hours later and by then I was ready to blow my head off.

"It wasn't like I was playing golf all day," David points out.

"Of course you were not playing golf. It's not what you were doing. I knew that you were at work, not playing around, but I was still mad."

"Mad?" he asks.

"Yes. Jealous, too," I say. "You got to get out. Get away. Away from the screaming, the fighting, the diapers, the juice, the snacks, the lunches, the laundry."

"You can stop now," he says. "I get it."

"You could come in, help, clean up, and be with the girls. You had nothing but patience, but I was running on empty."

"It's Jackson Browne," he says.

The boy knows song lyrics like I know metaphors.

"You know, the song 'Running on Empty.'"

"We can listen later," I say, sighing a bit.

The point is that on those nights, David was a much better parent to the girls at that particular time.

I needed to get out, do anything. It could have been a run, a short visit and glass of wine with Amy across the street, or even going to the grocery store. The "what" didn't matter.

"There were some nights I barely even got one foot through the kitchen door and you were blowing past me like a shoplifter running from the cops," David says.

"The house, the kids . . . I was being suffocated. I needed to get air, to put my oxygen mask on. Then, I could come home and be the mom that the girls needed me to be. And I could be more open and available to you. I could be the good me, not the other one. Bad Julie."

"Sometimes I like Bad Julie," David says.

As if I didn't know.

"Not that 'Bad Julie,'" I say.

"No, that is for sure. And I hate to use the word plagiarize, but isn't this oxygen mask the same thing as that guy who wrote *The 5 Love Languages* talked about?"

"So, you did read it?" I ask.

I have given him dozens of books to read over the years. They generally end up under some piece of World War II nonfiction.

"I did, yes," he says.

Well, how about that? Apparently, he was not paying close enough attention though.

"What Chapman wrote about in that book is a 'love tank,' not an 'oxygen mask.' He was talking about the need to be loved, and how love acted to keep one happier, more emotionally fulfilled," I say, trying to educate a bit.

"Love tank, oxygen mask. Still sounds like a bit of a rip-off to me," David says.

"Totally different, trust me," I say. "And we were talking about those times when the kids were little, you had been out all day working and I needed to get out."

"Get your mask on and breathe, so that you could be a better mom."

"Right."

"It's not like you were winning any wife of the year awards either," he points out.

Nope. And I knew it.

"It's the same thing for you and me. I just did not have it in me to be talkative, friendly, sexy, whatever you wanted me to be at that time," I say.

"So, you left."

"Exactly. I left, put on my mask, and was able to breathe again," I say. "I could come home and be a better mom to our kids. A better wife to you."

"I guess I should pay more attention the next time we get on a plane," David says.

The RV

"You have got to give some rope. A comfortable amount is all.
We don't want anyone getting hanged."

—Julie

A few years back, David wanted to buy an RV. We went all over the area, looked at different ones, and drove a few. He even talked me into driving a thirty-five-foot Winnebago even though I was scared shitless behind the wheel of the thing. At home, we binge-watched several of the cable RV shows, *Going RV, Big Time RV,* and others I just don't want to remember. On one visit to a dealer near Thurmont, Maryland, the dude was ready to plunk down a deposit on a particularly snazzy class A rig. (See, I even learned the lingo.)

David thought it would be fun, a good way for us to spend time together, take the kids and grandkids, do things we had not done before. Plus, he liked to say "re-cre-a-tional ve-hicle."

The whole RV search led to some funny exchanges between the two of us.

"DB, you really have never been camping," I say.

"Nope," he admits.

"You hate traffic."

"Yes."

Admission number two.

"You like bourbon."

"Now and again," he says.

"Drinking and driving a six-thousand-pound house on wheels probably does not bode well," I say.

"Probably not," he agrees.

Frankly, that should have been the end of the discussion. A guy who doesn't like traffic, who never really went camping, and who likes to drink when he relaxes certainly should not be in the market for an RV. Add in the fact that he would have to change those gross water tanks (the gray water, the black water . . . I can't even think about it). The thought of popping into Walmart RV stations from Arkansas to Wyoming to change water tanks and hook up for the night made me cringe.

"I'd buy you some orange juice and beef jerky before heading back onto the road each morning," he says. "And if you're really lucky, maybe a sexy pink Metallica sweatshirt."

I tried to give it serious thought. I really did. But it didn't compute for me. My deep-in-his-50s husband who can't fix anything but a cocktail bellying on up to the Walmart RV station to dump his doody water just did not seem like a reality I wanted to experience.

The fact was, however, that the RV was a symbol of something. Something he had to go through for himself, and I didn't want to be the one to throw black water on his ideas. All those years he spent coming home after work, hanging out with the girls, doing homework, games and coaching and parties and carpooling on weekends were over. Now that those responsibilities were pretty much done, he was looking for something else. He was searching for something new to fill his time.

And the funny thing of it is this—he thought I wanted one also.

"You looked great behind that wheel. We were going to go to the RV show in Hershey, remember?"

I did remember. I would have gone, too. If I had to.

"It was kind of a pivotal time for you," I say.

"I'm not sure I would call it 'pivotal,' but yeah I suppose you're right," he says. "I did want a new challenge, a shakeup of some kind, whatever."

"I saw you were searching. You needed me to support you," I say.

And I did support him. Right up to the point where he wanted to hand over a credit card for a down payment to hold a thirty-five-foot Winnebago. That's where it ended.

"A team player is what you mean?" he asks.

"Sure, but I don't mean it in some sort of martyr-like way. I mean I did it, I went with you, got interested, watched the shows, all that stuff, not because I really wanted one or could see myself in one," I say.

"Like faking an orgasm?"

"That's about right," I say, "but with a more significant investment."

He was quick to point out that I wasn't the only one doing the supporting over the years. I knew what was coming next.

"How about that 'Julie-Art' stuff?" he asks.

Yep, that was it.

"All those trips to Michaels for rope and plastics, canvas and frames. You have to admit. Those paintings were awful," he says.

They were not paintings. They were wall art. But he had a point. We had two kids. I couldn't really work much with him putting in sixty hours a week at the office. I needed something different, something else to put energy toward. And David supported me, even if it was junk. He did it because he loved me. He supported me. And it helped. We are thirty-three years and counting.

"You don't really fake orgasms, though, do you?" he asks.

Me? Never. I want him to be happy.

I Don't Give a Shit about the Dry Cleaning

"What matters to you may not matter to her. Want to do something nice? Do what your partner will think is nice, not what you would want him or her to do for you."

—*David*

Julie is not much for affection or flirting. We don't do a lot of hand-holding and I swear that I could shave my head, paint my face blue, and wear the same shirt to work each day for a week and she wouldn't notice. She does, however, pick up my dry cleaning.

"That's my way of expressing affection. Doing things for you," she says.

The fact is that I couldn't care less about whether she picks up my dry cleaning. I mean, I know she is doing me a favor, and while I appreciate it, I can get the dry cleaning myself. It's not that big of a thing. If I could swap the dry cleaning for something else, say, getting noticed, I would do it in a minute.

"For what? You wear the same jeans and T-shirt every weekend we go out," she said.

"I have a lot of different T-shirts, so I don't see how that should get in the way."

"It's different for women," she says.

"I'm calling the political correctness police."

"Can't wait. Love handcuffs," she says.

Handcuffs? Sure. Big talker, that one. What she is missing is that it isn't different. Most men who have been married, in a relationship for a while, who are getting older, we want to be noticed for how we look, not what we do or what we need to do.

When we have this discussion, she tells me I am whining.

"That again is where you are wrong. And that is because you don't see it or refuse to. You want me to be happy, feel good about myself, about us?" I ask her.

I know the answer. She wants all of those things.

I don't want her telling me about the work around the house that she needs me to do, the errands I need to get done, and when those things are done, expect that patting me on the back and thanking me for doing them somehow makes me happy.

"So, let's just say we do have things that need to get done. How do you want me to ask you to do them? What should I say that helps to accomplish those things?" she asks.

"First of all, actually take a second to pull your head away from the computer screen and look at me before I leave for work or when we go out on a Saturday night. Tell me I look good, that you think I'm sexy; you're attracted to me. It's not all that complicated." Says me.

"You want me to lie," she says.

Actually yes, I do. If that is what it takes.

"I'm kidding. Really, I am. I don't need to lie," she says.

We go on about this all the time. It's important to me. So why can't my wife bring herself around to say those kinds of things? I know she loves me, but love really isn't the point here.

"I know the point. Believe me, I get it. The point is you are insecure. I mean, come on," she says. "We have been married for more than thirty years, together for three or four before that," she says.

Exactly. I'm not twenty-five or thirty anymore. Just because we have been together for all that time doesn't mean she should ignore me, not notice anything.

She tells me that she does notice.

"So, if you do notice, how hard would it be to tell me? Takes a few seconds. A lot less time than getting my dry cleaning."

"Again, it does not really cross my mind during the day-to-day of things. You should know that I notice, by what I do, not what I say," she says.

Really? Why should I? The fact is that half the time I think I could be anyone. Walking around the house, taking her to dinner, watching TV, whatever. So long as it's my voice she hears, I seriously wonder if Julie would notice if it were someone else who dropped into bed next to her.

"I would notice if it was Keith Urban," she says.

I have no doubt she would notice if her hall pass got in bed with her. Okay, so bad example. The fact is though— and in my business I see it every day—people in relationships can get complacent. Complacency leads to boredom; it leads to taking your partner for granted. In a relationship, nothing good can come from either. All of that often leads to anger, frustration, and cheating, just to name a few.

Julie is quiet, trying to appear to be listening carefully to my feelings. I know the truth.

"You're thinking about Keith Urban, aren't you?" I ask.

She denies it, but I know the truth. I keep going anyway.

It just should not be difficult to notice your partner and, like I said, I am one hundred percent sure that there are millions of others out there who feel just like I do. People come into my office every day who have had extramarital relationships. It is a common thread. "She doesn't notice me." "He doesn't make me feel good about myself." I can't tell you how many times I have heard those phrases from people sitting across my desk.

From my vantage point in the world of divorce, the truth is that, for the most part, human beings are not all that complicated. I am not that complicated.

"Okay, I will try to be better about saying I love you," Julie says. "And Keith Urban has passed fifty also, by the way. DB, I love you. You're so handsome. You're so sexy. I can't keep my hands off of you, big boy. I want it. I want it now."

Is she lying?

Do I care?

Silence Is Not Golden

"Do what our pets do. Dogs bark. Cats meow. Humans need to speak."

—Julie

We have been together a long time, DB and me. We have argued, yelled, walked away from each other. But you want to know what really upsets him? Gets right at him, is hurtful in a way that nothing else can be?

"The worst? No sex for more than a week," he says.

That's not it. It's the old standby. The "silent treatment." He just hates when I won't speak to him. I'm pissed, he wants to talk it through and, in a role reversal, it is me who is just not interested.

"That *is* the worst," he says.

The truth of it is, the silent treatment is not at all healthy in a relationship. Here's how it goes. DB does something to really piss me off. Instead of talking it out, fighting, screaming even, I just shut down and don't talk to him for hours—sometimes even days. I have had couples in my office that have gone weeks without talking to each other, passing by in the kitchen or the bathroom, on their way to work. Not a word.

"Does any of this sound remotely familiar?" I ask.

People need to talk; even assuming one of them is one hundred percent wrong. Let's assume, for example, that whatever he did is not life threatening, not cheating, not murder, arson, or any other criminal act. He says something mean, does something he shouldn't, something along those lines. His wife is mad, she is upset at him, and she is entirely correct. Not even a close call. Whatever he said, he did, he shouldn't have. Take that as a given.

"She doesn't tell him that she is mad?" David asks.

"No."

"And she doesn't yell or scream at him?"

"No."

"Does she throw his golf clubs out the window?"

I did that once. Not out the window, actually. I threw them down our driveway. A distinction without a difference, I suppose.

So, what's wrong with her not talking to him? Better than yelling, screaming, even destroying his property, no? I don't think so. Not being spoken to for any length of time is just a bad feeling, a you-are-dead-to-me feeling. As if she is trying to exhibit some sort of power, control over her husband. At its essence, she is punishing him. While a ten-minute time out might be fine for a five-year-old in the midst of a meltdown, I don't see a place for punishment in a healthy adult relationship.

If communicating leads to connection, something I talk to clients about each and every day, then the converse of that—not communicating—leads to the opposite result. Disconnecting.

Many of us are old enough to remember *The Flintstones* cartoons. Those folks at Hanna-Barbera were smart, they reran the same theme in many of the half-hour shows. Whatever the circumstances, Fred did something wrong. He was apologetic. He knew he should not have done what he did or said what he said. In almost every episode, Fred got into trouble. A day or two in cartoon time would go by and his wife Wilma would still not be talking to him or, even worse, simply to tell him to do something, maybe not to forget to do something. What she says is in a frigid, distant voice. Dismissive. Disconnected.

It works the same in real lives. People don't talk in the morning or at night when they are brushing their teeth. No calls or texts to the other from work during the day and certainly, no "goodnight" or "love you" before the lights go out. Now the spouse getting the silent treatment is angry, too. Just like Fred did, our real-life husband decides he won't talk to his Wilma either. More time goes by. They continue to avoid, ignore, and not speak to each other.

"Someone has to apologize, someone has to end the impasse," David says.

David is right. Someone does have to step up and break the tie, so to speak. When that happens, the silence probably ends. But I think that the damage to the relationship remains.

"Wilma would have been better off breaking a few golf clubs," David says.

It's Not What You Say, It's How You Say It

"The medium really is the message. Ignore the medium and the message doesn't get through."

—*David*

Of all the arguments Julie and I have had over the years, without any reservation I can say that most of them have not been about what one of us has said but rather how we have said it. Or, more specifically, how she has said it.

"I see. You're innocent in all of this," she says. "Why me?"

Why her? Because I am usually nice.

"Mm-hmm. Were you nice when I pointed out a guy that I knew from college over at The Boathouse the other night and you asked if I had slept with him?" she asks.

It was meant to be a joke. Didn't work out that way. I apologized.

"I did, by the way," she says.

"Did what?"

"Sleep with the guy."

Good to know, I suppose, but the issue is how we, how other couples, talk to each other. In our relationship, it is fair to say that I am the one more bothered by Julie's tone than she is of mine. It gets to me in a way that it doesn't for her and she is well aware of how her tone, sometimes sarcastic, other times demeaning, bothers and adversely affects my mood. And since she knows it's there, it strikes me that Julie should be more cognizant of it. Be a little more thoughtful in how she says something. The critical comments in and of themselves don't bother me if they are expressed in a decent way. It's when she hits me with that "you are a six-year-old" kind of attitude that bends me over and makes my head explode.

"My poor little lawyer," she says.

My sensitive social worker wife.

She asks for specifics.

"Remember when we were at the beach a couple weeks ago? I was packing the cooler," I say.

"That ridiculous Yeti thing?"

"Yes. That ridiculous Yeti thing. Can I finish?"

"Okay, but I still don't understand why a cooler cost that kind of money," she asks.

"It keeps everything cold." It does. It's amazing.

"Imagine that. A cooler that keeps things cold," she says.

"It works for days."

"Like you would leave a sandwich or a beer in your cooler for days?"

"Can we move off the Yeti cooler? Can I finish my thought yet?" I ask.

Whenever I am the one that is pushing to make progress, it seems she plays the class clown.

So, anyway, I was packing the cooler and Julie asked where the fruit and cheese were. I had put them in a plastic bag from CVS. She went right at me. It was like I had flushed a hundred-dollar bill down the toilet.

"Why wouldn't you put that in your fancy cooler? It will go bad," she said.

"Your tone was condescending. You looked at me like I was that cross-eyed Banjo-playing kid in the movie *Deliverance*. Like I was a moron," I say.

"It was stupid. The food would go bad. That's what that cooler is for, after all," she says. "Why in the world would you ruin food by keeping it in a plastic bag for hours in 90-degree heat when you could have put it in a cooler that costs more than a car payment? What should I have said?"

What should she have said? My socialist, left-wing therapist wife? Maybe something like, "DB, you should probably put the food in the cooler, not the beach bag. It might go bad." That would have gotten her point across, I would have taken out a couple of the beers in there, moved things around, whatever, but I would have put the food in. And that would have been the end of it.

"Instead, I got pissed at how you spoke to me and was angry for about an hour or so after," I say.

"You don't think you are too sensitive?" she asks.

Maybe I am.

"I understand your feelings got hurt, but really you are asking a lot of someone to have to constantly formulate the specifics of how to say something, or ask a partner to do something," she says. "Some things just come out."

She is right there. Some things do just come out before we can process and think about what we say. I get that. Maybe the better play is to avoid criticizing or correcting your partner in a way that you know will scrape him in a particularly sensitive way. A way Julie knows will make me angry and defensive.

"Like comparing you to a certain relative when you start feeling sorry for yourself?" she asks.

Instead she should remind me of something positive, a reason I should not feel the way I do.

"See, that is a specific thing that I can avoid. And, I think, most people can do better with a clear 'don't do this' as opposed to an all-encompassing rule for behavior," Julie says.

If she knows that's a 'hot button' kind of thing for me, then it's easy. She should avoid it, tell me what she wants to tell me, what she wants me to do, just but be a little nicer about it. And I can tell you it happens all the time in relationships all over. If people were nicer in how they spoke to their spouse, partner, whatever, couples would do a lot less fighting and there would be a lot fewer divorces.

"Fewer divorces? That wouldn't be good for business," Julie says.

"That's okay. I would do something else. Be a tax lawyer. Estate planning. I don't know."

"You are such a Good Samaritan," she says.

"Thanks."

"Me too. By the way, I loaned your Yeti cooler to Amy."

If It Won't Matter, Don't Say It

"Sometimes the best thing to do is nothing."

–Julie

For whatever reason, and David jokes that it has to do with alcohol, we just don't argue or fight very much. There was a bit more antagonism and arguments earlier in our marriage over money, finances, kids—the usual—but really not all that much even then. So, is it the alcohol? Maybe drinking has been a key to our relationship.

Of course it hasn't.

"It may not be the only key, but it's definitely on the ring," David says.

He is serious.

"Really, I am. Having a drink together is relaxing for us. It's a way to just sit back, look back on the day, talk about what happened, and bounce things back and forth," he says.

That does raise a question for me. "We *can't* do that without a cocktail?" I ask.

"Sometimes, no," he says. "I am really not interested in hearing about the kid who shits himself in math class or the father who emails you sixteen times because his twelve-year-old isn't working hard enough to get into Harvard or MIT or wherever. World is coming to an end. His kid will have to make his way through college at Michigan or some other third-rate university like that."

My husband is going to hell.

"Really, though, you know I am interested in what you do and I like hearing about your day, what happened and all that. Most of the time, anyway. It's just that I am a much better listener if I am drinking while you are talking."

Okay, I can live with that. I ask him to refill my wine glass.

"That's my girl. Same vintage? From the box?"

"Nothing wrong with wine in a box." It's true.

"Full glass, half glass?" he asks.

"Big-ass glass. And while you are pouring, tell me this. If alcohol is one of the keys on the ring, as you said, what's another?"

"Lots of them. It's a big key ring. Like a school custodian," he says.

And he says *I* use a lot of metaphors. "Just one. Let's stick to one," I say.

"Easy. Knowing when to keep your mouth shut."

I wonder whether he is talking about a client on the witness stand or a person in a relationship.

"Works for both actually. But we are talking about relationships. The keys and all that."

Keeping your mouth shut does not seem like a particularly sophisticated strategy for maintaining peace in a relationship.

"It doesn't have to be sophisticated. It works. I've been doing it for years," he says.

David fills me in on his prize strategy; one of his keys to a happy marriage. Silence.

"Understanding that if what I am about to say won't make any difference whatsoever, I just don't say it," he says.

I am a therapist. I help by talking. This doesn't sound like good communication to me or a key to anything but strife.

"So, if you don't say anything, what do you do instead?" I ask.

"I drink."

"Brilliant," I answer.

It's not all that brilliant, actually.

"Indeed. Really, I do. I just keep my mouth shut. Don't say a word," he says.

I'm looking for an example, some identifiable moment in our relationship where his "keep my mouth shut" key was used to turn a lock and avoid conflict.

I should have seen it coming from a mile away. The Jeep Commander.

Jeep came out with the Commander in 2006. It was a Jeep with three rows of seats and would fit our family comfortably. I could dump the minivan. DB told me to wait, that we should put a few more years on the minivan and then get the Commander. I didn't listen. I had to have it. I went out on a Saturday and bought it a couple of months before a planned drive with the girls to visit family in Florida.

Maybe a month or so into driving the Commander, I got this terrible feeling. The Commander was hard for me to drive and the visibility was awful. I could barely see out the rear window over that third row of seats. It was cool to look at but that was about it. I came home one afternoon and told DB that I couldn't get it out of my mind. Night after night I woke up thinking about it. We were going to get into an accident and all be killed on the way to Florida. I should never have bought it and now I needed to get rid of the thing.

"Two months, maybe a thousand miles on the thing. Cost us thirteen thousand dollars to get out of it on a trade. Good investment," David says.

I remember clearly how patient he was about it. He didn't raise his voice. In fact, now that I'm thinking about it, he didn't say much of anything.

"That's my point. I was pissed, but I didn't say anything," he reminds me. "If I had said no, you have to keep it, then what would have happened?"

"That's easy. I would have taken it in when you were at work and traded it anyway," I say.

"There you go," he says. "Plus, you felt bad enough about it. I didn't need to pile on any more guilt by adding my two cents. Instead, we had to concentrate on finding another car, one that you wouldn't have nightmares about driving. A relationship isn't going to work if it's about scoring points against the other person. There's no 'I' in 'team' and all that."

I'm proud of him. This is a real teaching moment for the impatient whiskey lover.

It does work both ways. When DB wanted a motorcycle, I didn't want him to get it, but didn't fight him over it. I knew this was something he was going to do so it made no sense to tell him not to.

"And when you always have to pee right before we go out, even though you could have done it ten minutes earlier, I just wait," I say. "I don't complain or ask why you didn't pee before we are walking out the door."

"And if you did, it wouldn't matter. I have my routine, so you let it go," he says.

I am a good wife. And DB is a good husband.

He refills my glass.

I Think I Can, I Know You Can

"Both of you need to push up that hill."

–Julie

Sometimes I think our relationship is a lot like that kids' book, *The Little Engine That Could*. You probably remember the story; a stranded train needs to be pulled over a mountain after its engine breaks down. The train asks several others to help it climb the mountain to the other side, but none of them will help. The little blue train, in our copy of the book, portrayed with a young, childlike face, jumps in and offers to help. Despite the odds, the little train pulls the large one up and over, all the while repeating the mantra "I think I can." The book is a story of optimism and hard work and our little girl Zoe just loved it.

"I think we read it to her about six thousand times. Gave me PTSD," David says.

"Well, I was thinking, we are like that book," I tell him.

"You and me?"

"Yes. And why we have been able to stick together when other couples haven't," I say.

"I thought it was because I know how to go places," David says.

He does know how to get around. My husband can find his way around, up, down, and through any city, town, forest, field, or wherever. And he doesn't need GPS.

I read in the book *Understanding the Divorce Cycle* that the risk of divorce is 50 percent higher when one spouse comes from a divorced home and two hundred percent higher when both spouses come from a divorced home.

"But what does that have to do with *The Little Engine That Could*?" David asks.

The train believed in itself and because of that it was able to get up the hill. People can be like trains, I think. If you believe you can do something, there is more likelihood that you can. When you put that together with the divorce statistic, it makes sense with couples, too.

"In other words, if you think you can get through a difficult time, you can?" David asks.

I think that is right. Let's say you have two people; one or both of them come from divorced parents. That is the life, the environment they knew, grew up with, and understood, so it follows that those people are more likely to see divorce as the norm and put in less effort toward their own relationship. On the other side of the fence, some couples I think get that and try to avoid what they went through as kids.

"I can't tell you how many times I have heard a client say, 'I don't want my kids to go through what I went through,'" David says.

"Meaning?"

"Meaning they remember their parents' divorce. It was bad, and they don't want their kids to have to experience it," he says.

That can't be the answer, though. After all, those people are still in my husband's office; a divorce lawyer's office.

"It is ironic, in a way. By that point the person has given up on the marriage and the relationship but is still mindful of the damage that a divorce can wreak on a child," David says.

On my side of the professional world, I often get the opposite. I am seeing this couple that is having a lot of difficulty in their marriage, but they are trying to work through things together. The wife Molly's parents divorced when she was young. She has a lot of painful memories emanating from her parent's divorce: the shuttling back and forth between homes, her mom refusing to let her dad come in the house to pick her up, the two of them fighting over the phone. She is hell-bent on making sure that her marriage to Joel does not end up the same way.

In one session, Molly told me about an argument they had recently when Joel made some off-hand joke that he was going to the courthouse to file divorce papers. She flew off the handle at him even though he was making a joke of it. Joel was taken aback at first, but he better understands her sensitivity when it comes to divorce now and he apologized.

"Okay, but where does the train come in with these people?" David asks. "Or with us for that matter?"

"With Molly and Joel, they both want to work on their relationship. They fight and have problems, but ultimately their goal is to listen to the other and find a way to work through those problems," I say.

David and I are the same way. Even when I hurled his golf clubs into the driveway one afternoon more than twenty years ago, we ultimately circled around and talked about what happened and why. I understood how he felt, and he ultimately came to see my perspective on things.

"It didn't take a heart-to-heart chitchat to know how you were feeling. I knew that when I saw my putter bouncing into the neighbor's yard," David points out.

"Okay, but when we talked, you at least knew why I felt the way I did," I say.

"I did, and I promised to make sure not to do whatever it was that I did to cause you to assault my golf bag. Can't say as I remember what it was now, all these years later, but I do remember that I made an effort to fix whatever 'it' was," he says.

"You believed that we could fix the issue, and we worked together and did just that. It's *The Little Engine That Could* all over again. It's the 'I think we can' concept," I say.

I know we can.

Couple's Kickstarters

1. When was the last time you got angry with your partner? What did you do about it?

   _____

   _____

   _____

2. What acts of kindness matter most to you?

   _____

   _____

   _____

3. What are the last acts of kindness you did for your partner?

   _____

   _____

   _____

4. What aspect of you needs more attention?

   _____

   _____

   _____

5. What aspect of your relationship needs more attention?

   _____

   _____

   _____

6. What is the most frequent means of communication between you and your partner? Do you talk, or is it text or email? Does the way in which you two communicate need to improve or be changed?

   _____

   _____

   _____

7. Have you and your partner gone a period of time without speaking to each other? Why? How did that make you feel? What ended the standoff?

   _____

   _____

   _____

8. When was the last time you and your partner did something special together?

_____

_____

_____

9. Do you and your partner set aside time to spend alone together, without any distractions?

_____

_____

_____

10. When you and your partner argue, does one of you immediately consider breaking up or leaving?

_____

_____

_____

11. Are you able to use an argument as an opportunity to strengthen your relationship?

_____

_____

_____

THE SECOND CORE
Money, Money, Money

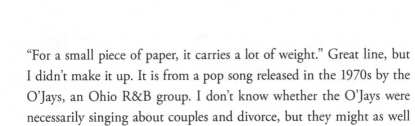

"For a small piece of paper, it carries a lot of weight." Great line, but I didn't make it up. It is from a pop song released in the 1970s by the O'Jays, an Ohio R&B group. I don't know whether the O'Jays were necessarily singing about couples and divorce, but they might as well have been.

For more than thirty years, I have listened to men and women tell me about the multitude of reasons that caused them to pick up the phone, punch in my number, make an appointment, and come to my office to figure out whether they should divorce, ask what would happen if they did divorce and, in some circumstances, look to have me talk them out of pursuing a divorce. Those first meetings, we call them "Initial Client Interviews," serve several purposes. I need to get basic information about the potential clients: their ages, when they were married, their educational backgrounds, work experience, and children, to name a few. And during the course of most if not all of those initial client interviews, talk of money makes its way to the forefront of our discussion. It might be that they don't save enough money or maybe even there is too much money, she's hiding money, he doesn't know anything about their money, she spends too much money, or he wastes money. No matter the theme, the concern, or complaint, it has been my experience that money and its tentacles provide many a spark for mistrust, arguing, resentment, and with a great degree of frequency, divorce.

Julie and I have had our share of conflict over money and finances. We went through a period, early in our marriage and when the kids were young, where we happily and naively took the attitude that "it's only money." We bought cars before the ones we had were barely broken in, houses we couldn't afford, and clothing and furniture we didn't need. After a period of living in that particular den of brainlessness for a couple of years, the walls closed and we found ourselves awash in debt and with more bills on the way.

To our credit, Julie and I got on the same page and made a commitment to save more, spend less, and get out from under the financial quagmire we had made for our family. We went on Julie's self-proclaimed "debt diet," eliminating discretionary buying, shedding ourselves of high car payments and crippling credit card debt, and clipping and using coupons at the grocery store (my specialty). We took family vacations at one of those places you get to stay for a dollar a week, provided you sit through a half day timeshare sales pitch. We "dieted" for a few years, but hell, it worked.

In fairness, Julie and I are fortunate that we are both educated and work in professions that, for the most part, have job openings. You don't often see a lawyer or social worker filing for unemployment. I recognize that not everyone is that lucky, but I am confident that our ability to communicate, to share, and take ownership—both of us—of the bad financial situation we were in gave us the springboard we needed to be successful in getting us to a better financial place. My sense is that I would have fewer of those initial client interviews if others did the same.

—*David*

Fun, Fun, Fun till Reality Takes Your T-Bird Away

"Buying it might feel good. Selling it? Not so much."

—Julie

My favorite color is teal. I love cars. For my fortieth birthday, DB bought me a retro-looking teal Ford Thunderbird convertible. In the winter, when riding in a convertible was not nearly as much fun as spinning around in seventy-five-degree sunshine, DB and I installed the teal hard top with round port hole windows on each side. The black leather interior was trimmed in—you guessed it—teal piping. That car was sweet. Gorgeous. To borrow a line from my husband, I could have had sex with that car.

A couple of years later, we had to sell it.

"I am still sorry about it," David says.

It wasn't his fault. We fucked that whole situation up together. We, not he, should have been smarter. We should not have bought that T-Bird, and we should have been a lot smarter about our finances and all that money we earned and should not have spent.

"I can never say no to you. It was a great birthday present," David says.

"It was but I shouldn't have asked. When I did, you should have said no," I say.

"No can do. You're too pretty. And I would do it again."

I know he would. I love him for it. The idiot.

It's more than just a car, though. It's about buying stuff we shouldn't have. A house that was too big, cars we didn't need, leather jackets, workout clothes, dinners out, etc. There came a point when owing all that money put a strain on things at home.

We spent too much and blindly assumed we would always make what we made for a couple of good years. When that stopped, when we realized we didn't have what we needed to pay for all the stuff we had already bought, with four kids, college coming, and one needing private school, we had to make changes. Going up was easy. Going down, not so much.

We fought a lot there for a while. I wasn't happy, and David was stressed and worrying all the time. His business was down, I was home taking care of four kids, and bills were piling up.

"But we put our heads together. We changed our habits. Made it work," David says.

We stopped a lot of discretionary spending, cut back, and got rid of things we didn't need. We started with selling my birthday present.

"I wish you wouldn't keep reminding me of that," David says.

"I'm still mad," I say.

Not at him. At us.

"We aren't the only ones, are we? Money causes a lot of trouble in a relationship, doesn't it? You're the divorce lawyer, you tell me," I say.

"It's one of the big four, yes," David says.

"Big four?"

This should be good.

"DB's four most frequent reasons why marriages break up," he tells me.

I'm ready for "DB's Big Four."

"Number one?"

"Sex."

"How did I know that would find its way in there?" I ask.

"Because it's one of the big ones. Word to the wise, lady."

"Yes, sir. And the others?"

"Two and three: finances and kids."

"And number four?"

"In your therapist world, what's the book, that encyclopedia of mental problems?" he asks.

That is the DSM. It is short for Diagnostic and Statistical Manual of Mental Disorders. It is a basic reference guide for mental health professionals. A bible of sorts, I guess you could say.

"My number four would be the equivalent of some diagnosis that no one can put their finger on," David says.

I think he is referring to an aspect of a mental health diagnosis that does not fit exactly into one of the diagnosis boxes.

You mean 'not otherwise specified,'" I say.

"That's the one. General misery and unhappiness. Not otherwise specified," he says.

My boy is creative. Funny, too.

In our situation at that time, it would have been better if one of us had been able to put on the brakes and say no. No, I can't have the car now, but maybe in a few years. No, he doesn't need a fourth leather jacket or another pair of jeans. Saying no would have avoided a lot of arguing and hard feelings. A couple not bound as tight, not as close, they might not have survived it.

"Those are the folks who end up in my office," David says.

"Business is good, I know."

"It has been," he says.

Maybe we can look at the new Camaro?

You Canceled
My Newspaper?

"Every little bit counts. Or does it?"

—David

The newspaper didn't come this morning. It won't come tomorrow or the day after that. My wife canceled my paper. What the hell?

"I just stopped the daily paper. You will still get Sunday, though," she says.

Should I be grateful that she discontinued my *Washington Post* subscription that I have had for as long as I have had my own address, and left me with only a Sunday edition? She didn't ask, didn't tell; I just walked outside and it wasn't there.

Julie gives me some rigmarole about the paper piling up when I am not home; no one else reads it and it goes directly from driveway to recycling bin. But really, why the hell does she care? I have been reading the paper just about every day since I was ten or so.

"You still can," she says. "You can read it every day on your iPad from wherever you are. No different."

To someone who gets her news from the early morning Facebook feed, maybe it doesn't matter. To me, though, it is different. I like it being in my driveway. I like the feel of a newspaper. If I'm home, I want it on my kitchen table.

"It's a waste of money when you aren't home, and if you can still read it online, what difference does it make?" she asks again. "The articles are the same, aren't they?"

They are.

"Everything is exactly the same. You turn on your iPad and you read the paper. No difference. And I just saved us about ten dollars a month. That's a hundred and twenty dollars a year," she says.

Sure. She has done some real budget cutting and saved us an earth-shattering sum. We can now both plan for early retirement on the ten dollars a month that isn't being spent for me to get my newspaper.

"Every little bit counts, doesn't it?" she asks.

Actually, no, every little bit doesn't count.

"Don't you remember when Sonny used to run down the driveway in the morning, grab the paper, and bring it back?" I ask her. Sonny was my first golden retriever, a rescue pup we adopted when he was about a year old. I loved when he went racing down the driveway in the morning, grabbed up the paper, and ran it back to me at the front door.

"It was impressive," Julie admits.

Sometimes when it rained, Sonny would get mixed up and get the neighbor's paper instead of ours. He was just as proud, a paper is a paper to a dog, after all. His mistake did, however, require me to throw on my coat, traipse down the driveway, and toss the paper across the yard into the neighbor's driveway to replace the one Sonny stole and brought to me. Great memories.

"Yes, but Sonny's been dead for twenty-five years," Julie reminds me.

For a therapist, she is not sending much in terms of empathy my way. She doesn't seem to get it. It's not just about a newspaper wrapped in a rubber band or stuffed into a plastic bag. It's about habit, about tradition. It's an irreplaceable part of my day, my life.

"Part of your life? You make it sound like I just strangled your best friend. Even so, I still don't know why we are going round and round over this. It is still part of your life and we don't have to pay as much for it," she says.

Time to go on the offensive. "Where were you yesterday afternoon?" I ask her.

"Why do you ask?"

"Just wondering," I say. I know where she was. She went to get Botox injections around her eyes. "How much is that again? Every time you go?" I ask her.

"About five hundred dollars," she says.

"A thousand dollars a year," I say, doing the math.

"Yes. But you want me beautiful," she says, smiling and flirty-like.

"What I want is my paper." I'm not budging.

"What does your newspaper have to do with my Botox?" she asks.

"Earth to Planet Julie. You canceled my newspaper that costs about a hundred bucks a year. You don't read it; means nothing to you. You want your Botox. That costs ten times as much. But that, you happily pay for," I say.

"Planet Julie is here and still does not see your problem," she says.

"With the money you will spend on Botox this year, I could get my newspaper every day for ten years. That's the problem."

Planet Julie thinks I am being ridiculous. "I just don't understand why we are fighting over not spending money you don't need to spend," she says. "I saved us money."

"You saved us a hundred dollars, getting rid of something that matters to me. You spent a thousand on something that matters to you," I say. I don't even understand why she needs the Botox.

"Because it makes me feel better and look younger," she says.

It's the same for me, metaphorically speaking.

"Oh, okay. Metaphorically speaking," she says.

I am being mocked.

"The newspaper doesn't make you feel better. You complain about what you read in the paper most every day anyway," she says. "And if you want to educate me to make sure I know what is going on in the world, you can do that without home delivery. Just read the news on your iPad and spout off at me about global warming, the Russians, whatever it might be on a given day."

I am trying. I really am. There is a bigger issue at play here.

"Bigger than newspapers and Botox?" she asks.

"It's that you did it, you took away something from me. You didn't ask me about it, we didn't discuss it. You just did it and that's it," I say.

She continues to bang the "I saved us money" drum. It is selective savings. What if I had turned off her credit card, somehow made it so she couldn't pay for her Botox?

"I would have used a different card," she says.

Maybe that was a bad example.

"We need to be done with this discussion," she says. "Just so I am clear, I should have come to you, asked if you would agree to cut off the paper, waited for you to say no, and then do it?"

"No. If I asked you not to, then you should have left it alone. We should have discussed it. And the fact is, you are right, I don't really need to have the paper delivered every day. I can read it on my iPad. Had you just approached me with doing it, asking, not making the announcement after you unilaterally decided it, we might have avoided all of this," I say.

"Wait. Hold on. What did you say?"

I don't know. I was on a rant.

"You said that I was right."

I don't remember that part.

"How do my eyes look?" she asks.

Learn to Drive before You're Sixty-Five

"Take your turn behind the wheel. It might be helpful someday."

—Julie

I was about ten years old when my grandfather Irving had a stroke. Irving was an active, busy man. He ran an electronics store, was handy around the house, and loved to drive. In fact, he loved it so much that my grandmother, Bessie, never drove at all. In fact, she never learned to drive. She didn't need to.

I remember vividly when my grandfather came home after a couple of weeks in the hospital; even at that young age I knew his life was forever changed. He could not walk, talk, or go to work. Obviously, he would never drive again.

Bessie was an amazing woman. Decades before it became the norm for women to go to college, my grandmother not only graduated college but also then went off to law school. She never practiced law and instead worked with Irving in the electronics store. She was quick-witted, smart, easy to talk to, and always interested in what was going on in my life.

With her husband unable to work or get her there, my grandmother had to learn to drive herself. She was sixty-five.

"It could not have been pretty, a sixty-five-year-old woman learning to drive for the first time," David says.

I remember it vividly. And no, it wasn't pretty.

"Being in the car with her literally scared the shit out of me," I say. "On the single lane roads, she drove so far to the right that one time I was able to reach out the back-seat window and grab a leaf off a tree as we went by."

Highway driving was just the opposite; she drove so slowly that I liked to count the cars as they whizzed by, honking and beeping.

"Lucky your grandfather could not talk," David says.

It probably was a good thing that he could not talk. I can only imagine what Irving would have said to Bessie as she motored her way through the highways and byways of southern Massachusetts.

"That lesson has stayed with me," I say. "None of us should let one person in a relationship handle all of something, whether it's driving or cooking or anything else."

"That's why you made me do that stupid ponytail test when the girls were little," David says.

Every so often when we were home, I would ask David to make a ponytail for one of the kids. I wanted to make sure that he could do their hair if something happened to me.

"It's the same when it comes to money," David says. "Many people come to me expecting me to help them 'get what's fair' during the divorce without having any conception of what 'fair' might look like. They don't know what they have saved or how much it costs to run their house each month. It is important to me that my clients, first and foremost, get educated about what it is they have. Only then can they have a decent sense of what they want, or what they need."

A client I have been seeing for some time recently lost her husband. We spent a full hour talking about how difficult it was for her just to go down the driveway and get the mail; her husband got the mail every day for the last twenty or so years. Since he died, she kept forgetting to get the mail.

"And when she did get the mail, she looked at bills that she didn't even know they had," I say.

"There is nothing wrong with a couple divvying up responsibilities," David says. "It's just that both should have a sense of how to do the other's jobs if they need to."

In other words, take turns driving.

A Balance of Power

"A balance of power between countries is thought to help avoid wars. Does it work in relationships also?"

—Julie

He is right. I didn't need that new pair of shoes. Both of us are past needing anything. I liked them and wanted something I could wear for work that was comfortable but cute.

"So, you are telling me that in your closet with a good hundred or so pairs of shoes, none are comfortable and cute enough to wear to work?" David asks.

Maybe it is a hundred pairs, maybe a few more. And no, I am not going upstairs to count them. What does he care anyway? He just got a new thing to put his golf clubs in. Golf bag, whatever it is. What was wrong with the other bag? Did the clubs need a new place to stay? He's being ridiculous.

"It's a travel bag. I will use it when I take them on a plane. It's got a hard shell and keeps the clubs protected," he says. "And, so we are clear, you bought the shoes because I got a new golf bag?" he asks.

That's not exactly what I am saying.

"What are you saying?" Another question.

"I'm saying that you shouldn't complain about me getting a new pair of shoes when you just got a new golf bag. And, by the way, I will get a lot more use out of the shoes," I say.

I have no idea why are we arguing about shoes and golf clubs. The entire discussion reminds me of a period, earlier in our marriage, when we dug ourselves into a financial hole, a good portion of which was a direct result of this very same "tit for tat" kind of thing.

It sort of went like this: David bought himself something. It didn't have to be anything even all that significant; maybe just a T-shirt or pair of sneakers. For some weird reason, his making that purchase pissed me off. Jealousy? Maybe a smidge, but I don't think that is the right word. I felt like things were difficult because money was tight, and if he bought something for himself, I should do the same.

"You are talking about a balance of power," David says.

I know little to nothing about history. What I do know, I have basically learned from my husband. Apparently, this "balance of power" thing is often a necessity in order for two countries to avoid going to war with each other.

"A balance of power is what helps to keep the peace," he says. "During the Cold War between the Soviet Union and the United Sates, both sides were concerned about keeping pace with the other; having equal amounts of weapons. A balance of power so that neither would have the advantage over the other. If it seems a bit incongruous, that is because it is. Arming up to avoid a fight."

I am not sure whether to recognize the logic of this whole "War of the Roses" kind of thing or be angry that my husband is comparing me to some warmongering country. But it was sort of the same mentality. Money was tight. He buys something. I have to buy something to keep up. And it wasn't just about buying things. Whenever David would come home from a couple of days away on a golf trip or some other weekend with friends, I would be mad at him. He would walk in; I would snipe at him right away, give him an "I'm off the clock" type of remark, and head out the door within about twelve seconds of his walking in.

I resented the fact that he left and was away for a few days. He was out having a good time while I was stuck at home taking care of the kids and dogs, cleaning, cooking, and doing laundry. And when the weekend was done, he seemed to bop on in, all refreshed, looking for me to be "Miss Happy Wife," and tell him how much I missed him.

"A blowjob would have been good too," David says.

That wasn't happening. None of it.

"It irritated me that you acted that way toward me," he says.

To be honest, in those days David could be out for an hour or two at the dentist or getting a haircut and I would still get annoyed. I would even resent his being in the bathroom for more than ten minutes.

"As a result, I stayed at work longer and ignored some things I knew you wanted me to do around the house. I got angry at you for being angry at me and I fought back," he says.

A tit for tat. A balance of power.

As the "arms race" continued, our financial situation got worse, the hole got deeper. We were fighting more and getting along less. Stress levels between us built up.

Luckily, we figured it out. We both understood that the other needed time, or needed help, or whatever "it" happened to be at a given time. The race, the contest, the "tit for tat" was replaced with a mutual understanding of what the other was doing, or not doing, on a given day, and what the other needed to feel better and improve his or her outlook or mood at a particular time. David started calling when he was on the way home from work, telling me to go ahead and go out when he got home. Make an appointment to get my nails done; go to the gym, whatever I wanted to do.

"And I wasn't as angry when you walked in the door," I say. Sometimes I even gave him a hug as I was leaving. Not too long of a hug. I didn't want him to notice my new shoes.

Don't Wait for the Repo Man

"Stay out of the dark when it comes to your finances."

—*David*

At least three or four times a year, I sit down with Julie and go over our financial picture; what we have and what we owe. She often rolls her eyes, pours a glass of wine, and sits down to listen or at least humor me. So, why do I do it? Why take the time to go through this exercise with a high likelihood that I will be ignored for most of the discussion? Julie really does not have a good sense of our retirement, where our savings are, how much we owe the bank for a mortgage or car loan, or just about anything along those lines.

"I make sure to tell you in the hopes that you listen to, I don't know, maybe half of what I say," I tell her.

She responds by telling me she listens to everything I say, all of the time.

"Really?" I ask.

"No, not really," she says.

She should. In my more than thirty years, I can't even count the number of divorcing clients who come into my office because they have separated and have no clue about what they have or what they owe. Sometimes they come in empty handed with no information, no knowledge, and no understanding whatsoever of their financial situation. Others come in lugging a couple of shopping bags stuffed with bank statements, torn bills, and a page or two from six different years of tax returns.

Julie asks for an example.

Just a week or so ago, a fifty-something woman, let's call her Tracy, hired me to represent her and try to negotiate a financial settlement with her husband's lawyer. She drove a Mercedes Benz, and lived in Bethesda in a house that she and her husband owned . . . or thought she owned, anyway.

"That doesn't sound good," Julie says.

It isn't.

During my first meeting with Tracy, I asked her, like I do with most people, to give me a sense of the family finances. Think about going to a bank and asking for a loan; I want to see her assets, liabilities, if things are titled in Tracy's name, her husband's name, or jointly. Sometimes people have assets such as houses, savings accounts, rental properties, etc. that are titled with other family members for one reason or another.

Tracy was totally in the dark. She told me about the house, the cars, and that she saw some statements come in the mail from Wells Fargo and a few other banks. Plus, she said they got a lot of mail from the IRS.

"That doesn't sound good either," my wife says.

"You are two for two," I say. "It isn't."

"Did she ask her husband about any of it?" Julie asks.

"No. She lived in a place that I learned about and named many years ago. I call it 'The Cocoon of the Uninformed.'"

"I like that," Julie says.

I like it, too. That's why I thought of it. Way too many people live that way, and trust me, it is not a secure or safe place to stay. Tracy was a long-term Cocoon resident.

"So, what happened with Tracy?" Julie asks.

Basically, Tracy went along in her cocoon for about fifteen years. She had a credit card to use, she knew the lights were on in the house, she shopped and bought what she wanted to, and the family went on vacations. She and her husband went to dinner on Saturdays. He worked late most nights, but she didn't give that too much thought. All seemed fine, until the Repo Man showed up.

"The Repo Man?" Julie asks.

Around eight one morning Tracy told me that she heard a couple guys hollering outside in Spanish, and a loud metal bang, something that sounded like a bulldozer. Tracy looked out and the white Mercedes with her *T's Benz* vanity tag was being tugged away.

"Oh, Jesus," my wife says.

I have her attention.

"Jesus had nothing to do with it. Tracy scrambled out the front door, hysterical, and screamed for them to stop," I say.

They didn't stop. Instead, the Repo Man and his associates laughed and yelled back at her, said a bunch of stuff, most of which she couldn't understand, and took off with *T's Benz* in tow.

"That's awful. Did she have any idea what had happened?" Julie asks.

"When she made out the word 'auction' from one of the repo guys, I think she started to get a sense of things, yes."

"Did she call her husband?" Julie asks.

She did.

"He apologized, told her they were broke, owed a ton of money to the IRS, and, oh, he wanted a divorce," I tell her.

At this point, I am doing my best to help, figure things out, and dig her out of the mess she has ignored by living in that Cocoon of the Uninformed for the last fifteen years of her marriage.

It's sad, sure. But she should have been more proactive, asked questions, and made sure she understood the family's financial situation. And believe me, there are a lot of Tracys out there. People who just live in the cocoon, don't ask questions, and don't pay attention, choosing instead to live their lives in a fog of blissful ignorance.

"With all the stress I see in families over financial issues, not to mention what we went through ourselves, I don't understand how people can be so in the dark," Julie says.

People who are staying together, in it together, they absolutely should understand the money side of things. And for those who end up on the divorcing side of the ledger, it can be even more important. Tracy could have saved an awful lot of money simply by knowing what was what, what they had, or didn't have, rather than paying me a few thousand dollars to figure it all out for her.

"I hear that," Julie says, leaving the room.

"I'm going outside," she says. "Want to make sure the car is still here."

Don't Bank the Bitching

"If you're angry and you know it, stomp your feet. And talk about it."

—*David*

"Another tough day on the divorce ranch?" Julie asks me as I walk in the door through our garage around six o'clock or so.

For me, just about every day is a tough day on the divorce ranch. People come in when they are in varying degrees of disrepair, so to speak. Some have not seen their kids; others want their spouses to spend more time with their kids. One husband found out about his wife cheating on him with a neighbor in the guy's basement just a block or two away from his own house. Financial stresses, problems, and shortages run rampant. So many folks show up in my office having had good solid careers, earned a good sum of money, but have little to no savings. And it is not because they didn't earn enough to save money over the years. The financial quandary that these folks face has little to nothing to do with what they earn. It's just that they spend too much, sometimes all of what they earn. They don't think of saving, what they might need later. Julie and I understand the mindset. We lived through it.

"It is. I read recently that about half of all Americans have less than a thousand dollars in savings," Julie says.

I find a curious divorce lawyer irony in that statistic.

"A lot of couples can't save money, but they can save up their complaining about it. Or, I should say, communicating about it," I say.

I have a client right now who has been married for almost twenty years. He and his wife don't have much savings, but that is only part of the problem. When he and I were talking, he got really exercised over his wife's spending. His face was flushing red; he was grimacing and waving his hands around all while telling me how she kept spending their money and didn't care about saving.

"Was he upset about one thing in particular?" Julie asks.

"No, and that's the 'saving' part that I am trying to explain," I say. "He spoke, literally, for over a half hour about it. He brought a big accordion file filled with credit card statements and receipts from as far back as ten years ago. Wanted me to understand her being a spendthrift, a shopaholic, whatever."

"Why did that have anything to do with his divorce now? What his wife spent ten years ago?" Julie asks.

"Not much, really. But he wanted to talk about it and, after all, that's what I get paid for."

"You've told me. Listening and giving advice that your clients don't listen to."

That is a fairly regular occurrence: me providing advice that I am getting paid to provide, and the person getting the advice ignoring what they are paying for. But that is another story.

As aggravated and upset as my client was about his wife's spending, he never talked to her about it. He stayed silent. More than that, he never did anything about it. She went to every Nordstrom sale; the kids had all the best and trendiest. The newest styles, clothes, sneakers, you name it.

Private school? Yes. Travel sports teams, overnight camps, and expensive vacations. And when each kid hit sixteen, they got new cars. And he never said anything to her. Not a word. He just boiled and bubbled up. It was about an eighteen-year boil. During that time, they spent all they had to buy things, then borrowed money, extended on their home equity line, and ran up credit card debt when they didn't have the cash.

"And instead of talking to her about it, trying to change and save money, he did nothing," Julie says. "Instead of saving money and talking to his wife about it, this guy just made eighteen years of mental notes of all her transgressions, hoarded all his concerns and complaints," Julie says.

"Exactly. He made his mental notes and got progressively angrier as the years went on. He kept those notes tucked away, didn't discuss them, instead putting them away and saving them up. What if he had talked to her about it at some point before things got too late? Maybe they would have had a discussion; maybe they would have had an argument. Could have been lots of discussions or even lots of arguments. Instead, he said nothing. He banked his bitching.

"That's a savings that won't pay for his divorce," Julie says.

Harvard

"Don't judge an Ivy Leaguer by the car she drives."

–Julie

I like to tell people that I went to Harvard. After the disbelief and shock wear off, they usually ask when I graduated. I didn't. I went to Harvard; I did, but just for a day when I was eleven. I was with my parents; it was for my dad's class reunion.

"Sounds like a great time. An eleven-year-old heading off to her father's college reunion," David says.

Actually, I can't really remember most of it. What I do remember were the cars. I remember wanting to see the cars. I know it sounds strange. Excited to go because I wanted to see the fancy cars that were going to be there.

"Why did you think you would see fancy cars?" David asks me.

At that age, I figured that if people went to Harvard, they all had to be smart. If they were smart, they had to be rich.

"And rich people have fancy cars," David says.

"Yes, and I love cars," I say.

My mom got mad at me. I got scolded. When I told her that I could not wait to see all those cars, she was strict in her response to me.

"She was mad at you for wanting to see the cars?" David asks.

"Not exactly mad. She was pretty firm, though," I say.

I can still remember what she said and how she said it. My mother was very emphatic. She told me that I was not going to see a lot of fancy or expensive cars at the Harvard reunion. She told me that people who went to Harvard were practical and did not need to prove anything to anyone. They didn't need fancy cars to try to keep up with others or feel important.

That whole conversation has stayed with me all of these years, even if it's not entirely true. She was right about the cars, though.

"What kind of cars did you see?" David asks.

"American cars, mostly. Chevrolets and Fords. A lot of Oldsmobiles," I say.

"Long gone, aren't they?" he asks.

"Oldsmobiles? Yep. For twenty or so years I think."

There were probably a few Cadillacs or Lincolns in the parking lot, but overall she was right. Nothing I can remember that stood out to me. And, really, it wasn't the lack of fancy cars at a Harvard reunion that I won't forget. It's what she was trying to tell me.

"Listen, I know your mom,'" David says. "She's smart and all that, but I don't see some hidden meaning in there. She just didn't want you to be disappointed when you saw a parking lot full of green Fords instead of a Rolls Royce or some such thing."

"Whether she intended to tell me something more meaningful or not doesn't really matter. She did."

"You mean the part about people who don't feel the need to prove things to others?" David asks.

"Yes, we see it all the time. Aside from the insecurity of it all, trying to keep up with others causes stress on a relationship," I say.

"Of course it does. If my wife . . . sorry, someone's partner, is upset that her friend just got a new kitchen, for example," David says.

It's not right, but he is right. David knew I wanted our kitchen redone anyway, then when Karen had hers done, I was a little sad.

"Sad, my ass," he says. "You were jealous."

"I was, and that was wrong. It made you feel bad, we spent money that maybe we should not have spent at that time."

"You loved it. Still do. It made you happy. And that was okay for me," David says.

"It did make me happy, but we had college tuitions coming. Broken air conditioners, toilets to be replaced, medical expenses. Other things," I say.

While we did eventually figure it out, I think if we had not been able to pay that debt, if it kept hanging over us, David would have gotten resentful and angry, directing both at me.

"So, what your mom was telling you, or what you think she was telling you, is that you don't need to be jealous about what others have." David says.

She was using it as a good teaching moment. Not just that we should not waste our energy being jealous about what others have, but that if you are lucky enough to have money or resources, you don't need to flash or show it off.

Or drive it around.

Cash and Kids

"Kids and money don't always mix. Have a few of the first, you often have less of the second."

—*Julie*

David was happy sticking at two children. But when Zoe's biological mom called and said she was pregnant again, that she was going to place that baby up for adoption also, there was just no way I could not take that child.

"I know. I can't say as I was with you on that one. Went along for the ride. As usual," David says.

I remind him that we got pregnant with Jo a couple of years later. He reminds me that Josie was an unplanned visit.

"Unplanned dessert, you mean," I say.

"I do," David says. "If we knew that all it would take to get you pregnant was to tear off your clothes and spray tan you in chocolate syrup, we could have saved a lot of time and effort," he says.

And money.

"Do you see this at all in the divorce world?" I ask.

"Covering each other in chocolate?" he asks back.

I ignore the latest attempt to send us down a sex path. What I am really interested in is if having kids, or having a certain number of kids, was a problem for couples going through divorce.

"Sure. People often disagree about how big their family should be, how many kids to have," he says. "Money is definitely a big part of it. There can be a ton of stress over how much it costs to raise a child today, between clothes and food and school. Daycare, and doctors, and dentists."

"Orthodontists and Ophthalmologists," I say. Those are two words not too easy to enunciate one after the other.

"I did see on CNN sometime back that it now costs the average middle-class family close to $250,000 to raise a child from birth to eighteen. And that doesn't include tutors or special needs costs or cars or prom dresses."

"I bet it's a longer list of costs not included than costs that are," I say.

"Divorcing parents fight about their kids' expenses also. It is one of the big negotiating points when I try to settle cases," David says.

I am a therapist. I am not exactly sure what he means.

"Usually when people get divorced," David says, "even for people who make good salaries, money can become more of a hot button issue."

It's not hard to do the math. There are now two households to support, two rents, and two sets of utility, cable, and other bills.

"And they are still making the same amount of money, I mean their incomes don't change, but what it costs to live, to support those kids, that grows exponentially," I say.

"Right. So, there is often a back and forth over how much each parent will contribute toward their child's uninsured expenses or extra-curricular activities, girl scouts and soccer and gymnastics. Allergy medicine, uninsured doctors' visits, shoes, and clothes," he says.

On my end, working with couples that are together, trying to stay together, it's not easy either. They are forced into making compromises or sacrifices. Often both. Maybe Dad can't play golf every weekend, and a spree at the mall will have to be a purchase at Kohl's or Target instead. The old car has to last a bit longer so we can pay for braces or eyeglasses.

In some families, only one of the parents wanted to have a child, or a second, third, or fourth. The other parent is pissed because now he can't do some of the things he wants to do.

"Presumably, they did 'it' together," David says.

"That is not always the case. I hear things like, 'we were fine with one' or 'you should have used birth control.' I see a lot of blaming the other for their situation."

"So, what can you do to help at that point?" David asks. "They already have the kids; they can't shove them back in or give them away.

"Acceptance and aspiration," I say.

"Sounds like some hoky-poky therapy strategy," he says.

"I wouldn't call it hoky-poky, but okay," I say. "I try to work with them to put away the feelings of anger or disappointment that they are missing out on something."

That is the acceptance part.

The second piece, the aspiration, comes next. I talk to both partners about aspiring to do one of the things that they each are missing out on. Say that Mom really wants a day at a spa for a makeover, manicure, whatever. The two of them work together to save money so she can get it. Of course, the kids still need what they need, so maybe it doesn't happen overnight. One day, he puts five dollars in the jar, two days later she does the same. After a few weeks, could be even a month or two, they have enough saved and mom goes and gets her spa day. Then they work on one of Dad's aspirations. Maybe he wants to be able to go to a concert in June and needs money for tickets. The two of them work together to try to get him to reach his aspiration.

This way, the couple is working together, rowing in the same direction. They both want the other to get what he or she wants instead of blaming the other for what they don't have.

The Swimming Pool

"Jump in. The water is fine."

—Julie

David and I often see things much differently. That should not be all that surprising as our "jump off" point for most relationship conflict is not at all the same. When someone comes to see me, it is most often to find ways to work on a relationship, improve communication, and make things better.

Conversely, "by the time that person has made it to my office," David says, "the relationship is usually skidding far off the ramp, past the point of no return, and the discussion centers on strategies and options for bringing it to an end."

Although the objective of our discussions may be dissimilar, the topics of discussion, areas of dispute, are often the same. Kids or sex or money, those are your big-ticket items, whether sad husband is looking to make his marriage better or trying to find a way to pull the plug. Money and different attitudes regarding how and when or even if to spend it, often wreak havoc in a relationship.

I have been seeing a young couple for some time now. Paul was raised in a working-class family and didn't have a lot growing up. He knows that since he and Jackie had a baby, their apartment is too small.

"Paul's norm as a child of having little to spend has bled into how he handles the family finances now as an adult," I say.

"So, he makes financial decisions based on what he has in the bank at a given time, what else he has to buy and save for, right?" David asks.

David has seen this kind of thing time and time again.

"I have a client with three kids and she is driving around in a small sedan or something like that, with no room for car seats, backpacks, or anything else the family needs to get around," David says. "Her husband knows they need a new car and is hell-bent on waiting until he knows that he can afford it, whether the existing car is safe for his family or not. It got to the point where he yelled at her for ordering a pizza, telling her it would be another month or more before they could afford the car. She finally had enough, took the kids, and moved in with her parents. Now his money is being spent on divorce lawyers."

With my couple, though, Paul won't even talk about it with Jackie. They have a two-year-old and need a bigger apartment, but he refuses to even look at possible new apartments online, much less visit a few.

Jackie grew up differently. She comes from a family with more resources, two cars in the garage, summer vacations, and kids in summer camp.

"Her family spent a lot of time talking about what they were going to do, where they were going to go, and how they were going to spend their money," I say.

Paul was distraught over how much she wanted to talk about a new apartment even though they were not in a place to get one. From his perspective, all Jackie ever wanted to talk about was their new apartment, when they would move, and the new furniture they would buy.

"Don't tell me. It made our girl Jackie angry," David says. "She liked the idea of planning because, after all, that was how she was raised. Paul shuts down, won't discuss it, and she gets pissed. How am I doing so far?"

"You are right on the money," I say. "Jackie went so far as to threaten him. She basically told him that if he would not even talk about this issue, something that needed to be discussed, that was important to the entire family, she would just leave with the baby and find someone who would."

"I hope you gave her my number," David says.

Not yet I haven't.

I told Paul to think of it like a swimming pool. Jackie wants to talk a lot about the new apartment and what they will need to buy when they get there. She is swimming. Paul won't discuss it, won't engage, and won't participate. He is on the deck, refusing to get in the pool.

"And all he needs to do is get in the water and try to swim with her," David says. "And by swimming with her, you mean he just needs to talk with her about it, yes?"

"Paul didn't grow up with a pool and isn't used to it. He needs to jump in, let her help him swim a bit, is all," I say. "Once she sees that he is in there paddling around a bit, she will feel better, knowing they are at least talking and thinking about something that is important to her."

"And what does Jackie do to work with Paul's fear of swimming?" David asks.

David is right. If Paul starts talking about the new apartment, he has done his share; he has jumped into the pool. It's not fair to expect him to keep talking about the apartment over and over again or for hours on end. Paul needs to tread some water for bit and then tell Jackie that he enjoyed the swim, but the water is a little cold and he needs to get out.

"Hope he doesn't drown first," David says.

Couple's Kickstarters

1. When was the last time you and your partner had a conflict over a purchase? What was it about?

   _____

   _____

   _____

2. Have you ever purchased something or spent money secretly, without your partner knowing about it? What happened when he/she found out?

   _____

   _____

   _____

3. Are one of you more frugal than the other? Does the difference cause conflict between you? How do you resolve it?

   _____

   _____

   _____

4. Were the two of you raised differently when it comes to money? Do the differences in upbringing affect your spending habits? Have those differences affected your relationship?

_____

_____

_____

5. Do you get angry when your partner spends money that you think he/she should not spend? Do you talk about it or keep it to yourself?

_____

_____

_____

6. Is your money "mine" and her money "hers" or is it "ours"?

_____

_____

_____

7. Have your spending habits as a couple ever caused a financial crisis? Did you discuss the situation without blaming or getting angry? Did one of you take it on as his/her sole responsibility or did you work together?

_____

_____

8. Do both of you know and understand your financial situation and circumstances?

_____

_____

_____

9. Do you complement each other with similar financial habits and goals or do those habits and goals diverge?

_____

_____

_____

THE THIRD CORE
Parents and Partners

Colleges offer classes in just about anything you can imagine. David jokes that when he was finishing up at Maryland, his toughest class was bowling (he somehow only got a B), followed closely by a couple of film classes. Take a quick glance through any undergraduate course book and you might find upper level offerings in rock and roll history, tree climbing and, at one Southern school, a student can earn two credits with a semester of underwater basket weaving. Unless you are a child development major, however, there is not too much out there to help us learn how to be decent parents.

Some time ago, I told David that all couples should be required to get some sort of parenting training before they have children. I learned from him, ironically, that in some states there are people who are in fact required to attend parenting classes . . . when they are getting divorced.

I see a lot of parents who struggle making the right decisions for their children, helping their children to make the right decisions for themselves, trying to figure out when to step in and help or step back and let their child go it alone. I tell folks that kids don't come with owner's manuals or twenty-four-hour tech support. You are often on your own. The best you can do is just that, the best you can do.

Of course, like anything else in life, our actions are often based on what we ourselves have observed or experienced. What did your mother do when you or your sister didn't come home on time? Did you get spanked when you were little?

Even professionals don't have all the answers. David and I had to get some help from a behavioral and child development therapist in order to try to better parent one of our children. Our third daughter was persistently infuriating, never listening, always testing. She wreaked such havoc in our house that no one wanted to be around her, her sisters and her parents included. I did my best to follow the recommendations. "You need to reward the good behavior, Julie," the therapist would say to me. "Ignore where you can, don't sweat the small stuff." It was good advice, and as a therapist I understood exactly what she needed me to do. And I did try, I really did. Not infrequently, though, frustration washed over me. It didn't matter what I ignored or what I tried to reward. My house was a war zone and my own child was the enemy. There were more than a few nights that David would find me despondent, soaking and crying in my bathtub; angry at myself for not being a better mom and at the same time dreading what was to come tomorrow.

I do think that, as a couple, a key to our being able to weather the struggles with Natalie was our ability to stay on the same page, at least on the outside. David and I had numerous disagreements as to the nature of her problems. Did she have mental health problems or was she just obstinate and oppositional? David usually fell onto the obstinate and oppositional side, while I searched for the right mental health diagnosis, along with the right medications to try to treat her symptoms. The key though, despite these frequent arguments, was that they essentially stayed between us. On the outside, for the most part anyway, we stood united in our positions, our communications with Natalie and our other children, and firm in the corrective actions we tried to implement.

Triangulation is a concept that was first introduced by a Swedish psychiatrist, Dr. Ernest L. Abelin, in 1971. Essentially, triangulation is a manipulation tactic used by one person against another by not communicating with that person and instead using a third party to do so. Have you ever heard the term "divide and conquer?" That is essentially triangulation. And kids can be masters at triangulating. How many times has any parent heard from a son or daughter that "Dad said it was okay" or "Mom told me I could stay at the party until 12"? My guess is that all parents have heard those types of things from their children repeatedly, over and over again, whether the child is a toddler or a teenager. Parents are regularly manipulated and played against the other. If they don't communicate directly to one another, the child's manipulation is a success, and the relationship between the parents can break down.

David and I were often victims of attempted triangulation by our children. We generally managed to be effective parents by sticking together, staying on the same page, and standing firm against the youthful but often effective efforts to divide and conquer us.

—Julie

The Adoption Option

"There are different ways to have a family."

–Julie

Not being able to get pregnant a second time was my first real challenge in life. Before then, the most difficult thing I ever faced was moving to Maryland from Boston when I was twelve, not knowing anyone and having to make new friends.

"Don't forget about summer school," David says.

He is referring to my, shall we say, less than stellar high school career. The University of Maryland would only accept me if I took two classes during the summer and got nothing less than a B in both in order to be accepted for admission in the fall.

Aside from both of those things, I really never faced much in terms of a struggle; I was outgoing and knew how to connect with people. I grew up in a good home. I had everything I needed and most of what I wanted. David and I met in college, got married, bought our first home, and got pregnant as soon as I wanted to. I really felt that all we needed to do was work at something to make it happen.

The "build it and they will come" kind of thing, David calls it.

Although both of our families were solidly upper middle class and better off than many, we were not like some whose parents took care of everything, bought them a house, or left them with a trust fund. We have both always been hard workers. No one gave us anything.

We are planners. There was nothing we could not accomplish, nothing we could not get, if we had a plan and did the work that the plan required.

"So, what changed when you couldn't get pregnant?" David asks.

That was the first thing that I could not plan for, work for, fix, or control. We had our first daughter Amanda, waited a couple of years, and were ready for a second baby.

"And all of a sudden, it wasn't happening," David says.

I went to doctors, had scans, treatments, a surgical procedure.

"Didn't we once have to have sex upside down, swinging from a tree?"

Although I have no doubt that my husband would not have hesitated to give it a try, we did not have sex swinging from a tree. We did try pretty much everything else, though, and it put a lot of stress on our relationship. I was sad; David was annoyed that I was sad.

"It was all you wanted to talk about. Why you weren't getting pregnant, what else we should be doing," he says. "Should you eat more protein, less carbs, exercise less? It was never-ending."

So, we decided to try infertility treatments.

"For about a tenth of a second," he reminds me.

"Do you remember the appointment with that fertility specialist after I had the surgery?" I ask him.

"I do. He already put you through that whole thing, they scraped out the endometriosis or whatever it was, and you spent two days in the hospital. It didn't work," he says.

"That led to the whole discussion about you giving me shots in my leg every three days, maybe harvesting my eggs."

"Do we have to talk about this?" David asks me.

"Are you kidding? You are feeling faint just talking about a discussion that happened more than twenty-five years ago?"

He hates anything about going to the doctor.

"Put your head between your legs," I tell him.

"I am. But it's a diagnosed disability. White Coat Syndrome," he says.

A big wuss is more like it. I think it, but don't say it. The guy is fairly muscled up for his age and has some mighty broad shoulders but passes out whenever he has to give blood.

"You didn't feel good about me being able to give you injections?" he asks.

No, not so much. I remind him to keep his head down.

"But it wasn't just that," I say. The whole process was out of our control. We were going to spend thousands of dollars and the odds were still against us that I would ever get pregnant."

I talked to David about the possibility of adoption.

I had a teacher when I was in high school who was really nice, sort of a mentor to me. She had two biological children and one adopted daughter. I loved all her kids, but had a special bond with her daughter. My relationship with that family gave me real positive feelings about adoption, even though I was only in high school. Those feelings stayed with me.

Unlike many people who want their children to be "theirs," David was on board from the minute I mentioned it. Some people feel that if they adopt, it won't be the same as having a baby biologically. The child won't have their hair or eye color, or otherwise look like them. There are also concerns that the adopted child will inherit his biological parents' physical or mental health problems. In other words, if my baby's mother was an alcoholic or her father had depression, is she more likely to have that too? They are good questions and when you are thinking about building a family through adoption, all questions that should be asked.

"Think about all the times someone said that our biological daughters Amanda or Josie looked like you or me or acted like one of us."

Our adopted daughters Zoe and Natalie didn't look like either of us, but in a bit of a twist, of all our girls Zoe is most like David.

Not that they look alike, but the two of them have tons in common. They both love theater, movies, and TV, and like David, Zoe is an avid reader and up on all that is going on in the world. "Really, though, the adoption process put us in control," David says. "We could decide whether to use an agency or not, how we would find a baby, whether we would go overseas or look only in this country. We weren't handing over a bunch of money to some fertility doctor and hoping for the best."

And David didn't have to give me shots.

Pass the Trash

"Sometimes you need to take turns. A quirky card game is a decent metaphor for doing just that."

—*David*

One type of poker my friends and I play during our monthly card game is called "Pass the Trash."

Here's how it goes. Everyone in the game is dealt seven cards, all down, like when Julie and I play strip poker. It starts as a "draw" game, not like blackjack or stud when some of the cards are dealt up so the other players can see.

"You haven't been able to get me to play strip poker in thirty years," my wife reminds me.

I figure that I am better off not reminding her of that one night during our trip to Florida a couple months ago when I had a particularly good run of cards after she had maybe one too many extra dirty martinis.

Anyway, "Pass the Trash" is a poker game, generally played with at least six people. All the players get their seven cards and decide which three they don't want to keep. Those three get passed to the first person on the left. Once everyone looks at their new cards, they then decide which two cards they don't want, and pass them to the person two seats away to the left. This goes around once more, so that after everyone looks at the two cards, everyone chooses one he doesn't want to keep and passes that one to the person three seats to the left.

Once all the passes are done, each player discards two of his seven and plays what is now a five-card stud game with the other five, with everyone turning over one card at a time, betting, raising, or folding in between. The high poker hand wins or it can be played as a high-low game where the best hand and the worst hand split the pot at the end.

"All very interesting, but what does this have to do with relationships?" Julie asks.

"It has to do with raising kids. You have to pass your kids, just like we pass the trash in the card game."

"So, in this weird card game world of yours, kids are the trash, is that what you are saying?" she asks.

That's exactly what I am saying.

"I don't think most parents would think of their children that way," Julie says. "Passing trash."

I don't mean the kids are literally trash. What I am talking about is passing the responsibility of taking care of a kid when you are tired and can't do it anymore. Can't do it effectively, at least.

"Like when one of our girls had a tantrum, something like that?" Julie asks.

"Maybe, but I was more thinking of the longer-term irritating, obnoxious, drive-you-crazy behavior from one of the kids that continues for hours on end. You know what I am talking about."

"Go on. You're on a roll, Mr. Therapist," she says.

"Happy to. After a full day of little Sally crying, screaming, challenging everything, Mom has just about had enough. She sends her to her room, the screaming continues, interrupts dinner, homework for others, things she needs to do around the house, so upstairs Mom goes—with one thought in mind . . . shutting that little shit up," I say.

"That's when as a parent you need to play my card game. Pass the trash. Get the other parent to take over. Don't go up those stairs. Go out for a walk, have a drink, watch some TV, but do not put yourself within ten feet of that screaming kid."

"We've both made that mistake," Julie says.

And we both felt bad after.

"I remember. We should have passed the trash," she says.

Voted off the Island

"Living with a child that has behavioral problems affects the entire family."

–Julie

David and I watched the first few seasons of *Survivor*, the television show.

"Sure, I remember," David says. "That obnoxious Machiavellian dude who liked being nude all the time finagled his way past an old former army veteran and some others to cash in on the million bucks."

I could not think of his name. My husband remembers all this kind of stuff.

"Richard Hatch. He was the only one who didn't get voted off the island. He went to jail a few years later. Tax evasion, I think," he says.

Looking back on when our kids were little, I think about that show and how it reminds me of us. "We were like the others, the ones who lost. It was like our family got voted off the island," I say.

We did not get too many invitations to go out for pizza or to Chuck E. Cheese with another couple and their kids. And family vacations, weekends to the mountains? Never.

"Mostly just the Mitchells," David says. "We got to go to their family's beach house."

He is talking about our close friends, the Mitchells. They were saints.

We did get invited one year to stay with my sister and her family at that timeshare in Hilton Head. It was a fun week, for the most part.

"I don't remember too much about that week except for the great tiki bar. Pool Bar Jim's I think it was," David says. "That and the 'kid in the creek' incident."

I am fairly certain that David and I both have post-traumatic stress that lingers from that afternoon, fifteen or seventeen years ago.

We were cooking out on some grills in the center condo complex, a short walk from the beach. There was a creek that snaked throughout the interior yards and wooded areas dotted with picnic tables along a path. It was a warm early summer night. David and my brother-in-law were cooking on the grill, kids were on the swings, and I was relaxing in an Adirondack chair, sipping a glass of chardonnay.

"I remember the scream," I say.

"I remember the splash," David says.

"The kid in the creek," he says.

"Natalie running away," I say.

"Smart move. She had shoved him in the water," he says.

The little boy—maybe he was eight—had some friends who helped him out of the water. Once out, he and the rest of the posse started chasing her. Natalie was screaming at the top of her lungs. High pitched, worse than nails on a chalkboard. Everyone around, parents, their kids, all of whom were enjoying their own family time, were now watching the event unfold. My daughter, the outlaw, was being hunted by a pack of third-grade boys.

"She was laughing too. That loud obnoxious laugh," David reminds me. "It sounded like a scene from *The Shining* but without the knife."

"The kid and his friends would have killed her," I say.

"I felt like killing her," David says.

He wasn't the only one.

"Lucky for her that her cousins were a little older than the would-be lynch mob and they grabbed her up before she got caught," David says.

Unfortunately, my sister was not so lucky. A couple of management people came, talked to her, and tried to get us all to leave. The only way we got to stay the rest of the week was by promising that Natalie would not come back.

When you have a kid with special needs, it can make life difficult, particularly one who looks (apologies for using a term that therapists don't really prefer) normal. What I am saying is this: when you met her, Natalie was fine. No issues. Every photograph looks like the rest of our kids. She seems to fit right in. No one would know anything about her mental health issues by looking at her.

"Remember how you used to say that it would have been easier in some ways if she were physically disabled? In a wheelchair or something along those lines?" David asks.

He is one hundred percent right. It would have been easier. People would have seen her and known that there was something wrong. They would have been sympathetic.

"They would have been nicer to her and to the rest of us," I say.

But she didn't need a walker, wasn't in a wheelchair. She had all of her hair. There was nothing to see, except how she acted. No one could see past that bad behavior.

And that is why we got voted off the island.

Make It, Take It

"Parenting is a never-ending relationship between cause and effect. The parent whose action (or inaction) causes a situation should also be the parent tasked to resolve the situation."

—David

"You ever play basketball at school?" I ask Julie.

"You have seen me try to play sports. What do you think?"

Julie is focused when it comes to fitness. She runs, rides a Peloton bike, and takes classes regularly at our local gym. But when the activity involves much in terms of coordination, that's when the bus stops. I was on a dance floor at a wedding once when she was trying to keep up during one of those awful "Cotton-Eyed Joe" line dances. In a matter of less than three minutes, she tripped over her own foot, hit an elderly fellow on the side of his head, and knocked over a decorative tree near the bandstand.

"But what about when you were younger? Like at recess? Didn't kids play basketball?"

"Some did. I didn't," she says.

"Okay, so here is a little education for you. Something you missed out on," I say.

She doesn't look up from her computer.

I start to tell her about how basketball games work on the playground. "Once you pick teams," I say, "there are two ways to run a playground basketball game."

Her head stays still, but her eyes rise, just a pinch above her reading glasses. "No one picked me," she says.

I knew kids like that. The ones who didn't understand that you had to dribble when you got the basketball, who would just go running down the court when you passed it to them. Those kids were left standing until no one else was left.

"I was the last to get picked for Red Rover, too," Julie says.

"Red Rover?"

"You know, the game where there are two teams on either side of the field, one person from one team calls a name from the other team, saying 'Red Rover, Red Rover send Julie over.' Julie then has to try to get to the other side of the field without being tagged," she says.

No balls to bounce or shoot, no particular coordination is required in Red Rover. "Why didn't you get picked for that?" I ask.

"I was slow. Also, I really didn't care about being caught. Not all that competitive," Julie says.

I started thinking about all the other sports we had to play in elementary and middle school. Dodgeball, volleyball, flag football, and softball.

"They made me play right field in softball. No one ever hit it into right field," she says. "That was actually my favorite. I could run out to right field, lie down in the grass, and not worry about anything until someone started yelling for me to get up because it was our turn to hit."

"So, anyway, in pickup basketball," I say, "there are two ways to play. One way is if you make a basket, then the other team gets the ball, like usual."

"And the other way?" she asks.

"Make it, take it."

Julie has no idea what I am talking about.

When you are playing make-it-take-it rules in basketball, when your team makes a basket, then you get the ball back—it's a reward for scoring. Your team gets to try to score again.

I think that the "make it, take it" rule can also be applied to parenting. "Instead of a reward, it's more like a responsibility," I say.

"I'm not sure what it is you make and what it is you take when trying to parent your child," Julie says.

"I was thinking about when our kids were little," I say. "Maybe I didn't put one of the girls down for a nap when she was two or three years old. She was being good, happy, playing. She didn't seem like she needed to sleep."

"But, a few hours later, you paid for it," Julie says.

That is exactly right. She was a mess. She should have had a nap but I let it go. Now, hours later, we had a screaming overtired three-foot tyrant on our hands. I created the monster; it was my fault. And one of us, at least one of us, had to deal with a screaming child.

"So, you are saying that since you caused that situation, it was your responsibility, or should have been your responsibility, to deal with her," Julie says.

"Make it, take it," I say. "I think parents get tied up, angry at each other when the other doesn't do a task or take care of something they should have, then try to dump the result on the other parent."

"Like if you had left that night to go play cards with your friends, sticking me with the screaming kid," she says.

"Like that, yes. If you as a parent create the problem, you make it, you should step up and deal with the consequences of that decision, you take it."

She smiles and looks at me. I came up with this all on my own. A parenting strategy that I thought of and she didn't. It seems to me that I deserve a reward.

"I made it, so now I want to take it," I say.

"Oh boy, here it comes," she says, knowing what is coming.

"Red Rover, Red Rover—send Julie over."

Jesus Joins the Family

"Is there a God or isn't there? Does it matter?"

—Julie

Neither David nor I were particularly observant when it came to honoring our Jewish customs, going to synagogue regularly or, in what I think is one of our failings as parents, doing much to teach our kids about the Jewish faith. We sent them to Sunday school and a Jewish preschool where they learned a bit growing up, but not much of what they learned outside of the home carried over into our home. There was a time, maybe for a year or so, when the kids got a bit older and the two of us tried going to services on Saturdays.

"We were trying to find something that could help us wrap ourselves around the Natalie situation," David says. "It didn't work."

Although the two of us were unable to find comfort or solace in the Jewish faith, our oldest daughter found religion on her own—a different religion.

"I still remember it like it was yesterday. Amanda coming in when she was sixteen to talk to us," I say.

She was very serious and sat down at the kitchen table and told us that she had something important to talk about.

I thought I was going to have a heart attack.

"And me, it all went right over my head," David says. "I was blissfully ignorant. I had no idea. I just thought she wanted a new pair of jeans."

"I know, right? Was she pregnant? Addicted to drugs? She wanted to get married. Maybe just gay," I say.

All these thoughts started swirling. I had no idea what could be so big and important that she had to announce her need to talk to us before telling us whatever it was that she had to say. She told us she believed in Jesus.

"She said she was Christian," David says. "I was glad that you started talking as soon as she told us because I did not know what to say."

"I remember talking and, in some way, I was proud of her."

"I really was taken aback," David says. "For me, it wasn't pride. It was weird. I can't describe it. Up to that point, she was just a kid. Our kid. That was really the first time that it hit home for me . . . she was growing up and thinking on her own."

"She was making her own decisions," I say.

"I guess that, for me, I didn't think that her first major life decision was going to be to change her religion," David says.

"It didn't come as that great surprise of a to me. The woman she worked for was a born-again Christian and a lot of her clients were as well," I say.

"You think she was looking for something that she did not get at home?" David asks.

"I do. We were never very observant, much less passionate about being Jewish. We didn't keep Kosher; we didn't celebrate all the holidays. It wasn't part of the fabric of our family," I say.

"And she told us that she was going to church and bible study. I just couldn't believe it," David says.

It wasn't that he was mad. Astounded is a better description. David reads a lot. He knows a lot about a lot of things. But his daughter was going to bible class? That was a tough one for him to grasp. She might well have said she was jumping on a rocket and heading off to Mars.

I took a more proactive and, yes, mature approach. I compared it to picking lipstick.

"I told her that if everyone around her was wearing purple lipstick, she probably would want to wear purple lipstick also, particularly when I just wore a nude, plain lipstick. No one gets excited about a nude lipstick, but purple is exciting and different," I say.

"So, you were comparing Jesus to a purple Maybelline," David says.

What I tried to do was talk to her, explaining that I thought the Jewish religion made more sense, was more reasonable.

"That's when we made the bonehead move and bought that *Judaism For Dummies* book," David says. "Once she saw we needed a 'For Dummies' book about our own religion, she was sold on Christianity."

We laugh about it now. In order to explain the underpinnings of the Jewish faith to our own child, we had to look at a 'For Dummies' book.

From then on though, we handled her newfound faith remarkably well. We didn't make it a big deal with her or ask her a lot of questions. It wasn't a nightly topic at the dinner table. There was no anger or yelling, and we didn't confront her, asking how she could have come to that belief.

"I think what was lost somewhere in the translation, what we didn't pass along that our parents did, was not the observance part. It was the association piece," David says. "I never really felt any kind of spirituality. I went to synagogue a couple of times during the year during the holidays, but there was no religious connection. But I always associated with being a Jew. There was never any doubt to me about that, it just didn't mean anything to me from a praying, faith kind of way."

"And I think that was the difference for Amanda. She had a space for that faith aspect of religion that you didn't have. Me neither, really," I say.

"So, you think she just saw us as very laissez-faire about it and therefore it wasn't worth her believing what we purported to believe?" David asks.

"Or not believe. Right. And while those feelings in her were growing, she was exposed to people who did feel strongly, did feel faith, and that faith gave them comfort," I say.

"Does it still bother you?" he asks me.

It does not. My daughter is kind, hardworking, patient, and a great mother to her own children.

"I look at it this way," I say. "I don't know what is right, who is right, whether Jesus is God's son, or some other guy."

David tells me that Jesus was a carpenter.

It doesn't matter to me that Jesus was a carpenter, nor does it matter to me what my daughter chooses to believe. It's the kind of person she is, the "who" not the "what" that matters.

No One Sends You Dinner When Your Kid Is in the Psych Ward

"If you are a parent of a happy, behaved, and well-adjusted child, then it stands to reason that another parent whose child doesn't fit that mold must be doing something wrong. Or does it?"

—Julie

A lot of things must go through a parent's mind when her son or daughter is admitted to a psychiatric hospital. A lot of things sure went through mine, but there is one particular memory I have about that first time that will never leave me.

"Which time are we talking about?" David asks.

Natalie was hospitalized several times as a teenager. I was thinking about the Dominion Hospital admission. David hated it there.

"It was a snake pit," he says.

I have seen my share of facilities, hospitals, and psychiatric wards. I understand how he remembers it that way. There were bars and buzzers, metal detectors and cameras everywhere. Except for the faux wood bed frame, our daughter's room was what you would expect it to be—a small box of gray and white. Natalie should have been at a friend's house, maybe watching a movie or sitting in our kitchen doing her homework and talking about boys. Instead, she was spending her days under lock and key, meeting with doctors, getting injections, and taking pills.

The fact is that she needed the help. She wouldn't listen to us and was wreaking havoc on everyone in the neighborhood. She broke into one neighbor's house, stole money from her friend's mother, and spray painted the sidewalk outside our friend's house.

"Don't forget school," David says. "The security guards there were probably thrilled to get a day off from chasing her around."

School guards weren't the only ones that were relieved. Our other daughters were happy to have a few days of peace.

"You and me too," David says.

"I know. It's all just so sad. One thing about that time still irritates me," I say.

I know he knows what I am talking about, but I keep talking anyway. "How many times over the years have friends we know been sick, when someone had to go to the hospital?" I ask him. "Think about just near where we live, or narrow it down even more to just our street."

"Plenty. I remember the one dad having that heart problem; his wife and the kids were at home. It was freezing cold," David says.

"Do you remember what we did?" I ask. I cooked them a meal—lasagna, salad, and dessert. Why? Because, that is what people should do for their neighbors and friends.

David remembers. "You took them all of those Milky Way Squares. None for me," he says.

He was trying to lose a few pounds.

"It wasn't like I was tipping the scale at four bills," he says. "One or two squares would not have hurt."

I wasn't the only one to take food over. I saw people pulling up in the morning on their way to taking kids to the bus stop, later in the afternoon, nighttime around dinner. All day long for days. They had meals for about a month. And even though the father was home in a few days, they still came. It did not matter. A neighbor was sick, and people wanted to chip in and help out the family.

"How about when the kids across the street got in that sledding accident?" David asks.

It was exactly the same. More meals for the parents while their kids were in the hospital. Just like with the other family, the good neighboring continued for a long time after the kids got home from the hospital. There were always cars out front, someone carrying a tray, grocery bag, or bottled water.

"You remember us getting anything when Natalie was in the psych ward?" I ask.

"Nope. Not even a Happy Meal," David says.

And everyone around knew she was in the hospital.

"So then, why didn't our family see the same outpouring of sympathy from the neighbors?" I ask.

"Can't say I ever gave it too much thought. I was happy not to have to talk to people, to be honest. I wanted to be left alone," he says.

"You were embarrassed?" I ask.

"Maybe. Some. Upset. I was a lot of things. None of which I wanted to discuss with anyone but you."

"If you were embarrassed, didn't want to talk about it, what do you think the neighbors thought?" I ask.

"That's easy. That we sucked as parents and had a loony tune as a kid," David says.

I don't think that's right, but maybe I should have asked it differently. "If you were embarrassed, if you didn't want to talk, and you were her father, how do you think the neighbors felt?" I ask him.

"I don't know how they felt. Not sure I really cared. I suppose that maybe they didn't know what to say to us," he says.

Yes. And that is why we didn't get lasagna.

I am not sure why that still bothers me so much.

As a therapist and someone who understands mental illness, it upset me. And as a mom with a daughter who was sick, it upset me.

Sticks and Stones

"Sometimes the stones hurt less."

—*David*

Raising a daughter who spent much of her young life in and out of doctors' offices, therapy sessions, being under constant watch at school, and getting grounded at home can be exhausting. It can be lonely. No one ever really understood a lot of what we were dealing with. With a few exceptions, our friends, family, neighbors, other parents all fell into one of two factions. It was either she was a bad kid or we were bad parents. Sometimes both.

"I still cringe when I think about the Rudmans' windshield," Julie says.

I wish she had not reminded me. It was like a Christmas miracle. We got invited to spend a weekend with friends and their families at a Christmas tree farm in the mountains of South Carolina. It was around the time of the DC sniper shootings in the fall of 2002. We were glad to get out of town, thrilled to actually be invited to spend a weekend with another family, and looking forward to having some fun with the girls at a place we had never been.

It didn't last long.

"First morning, wasn't it?" Julie asks.

She is right. It wasn't even noon on Saturday before the walls started to cave. Natalie started yelling and running around at the crack of dawn. She woke us, our other girls, and the rest of the two families there as well.

"Like most mornings, she was driving both of us crazy from the moment she rolled out of bed," Julie says.

"We were unpopular very quickly," I say.

It didn't take long for the fighting to start.

"I think Natalie was doing her usual, screaming, laughing incessantly, bothering the other girls, taking their things. At some point we were able to get them all dressed and outside," Julie says.

"We were going to go on a walk up the mountain and see the fields of Christmas trees," Julie says. "It was beautiful. There were horses, barns, and wide-open space for the kids to run around. You remember any of it?"

I remember the broken windshield. Not much else.

We got outside, there was some more arguing, Zoe yelled, Natalie screeched, and then I remember hearing something whiz past me and into the minivan. Having had enough, Zoe picked up a rock and winged it at her.

"Smashed the Rudmans' windshield into smithereens," Julie says.

We spent the rest of the day calling around auto body shops in wherever we were, South Carolina, until we could find someone who would replace it for them.

"It cost us six hundred dollars, didn't it?" Julie asks.

It cost $606 to be exact.

I felt indescribably miserable. Even though Julie was there, I felt alone, on the outside, sticking out in a crowd. Two of my oldest and closest friends and their families were away with us on what was supposed to be a relaxing and enjoyable weekend with our children. It was like I had this huge pimple on my nose and everyone was staring at me.

"And what about the kids? If you felt that way, I can't even imagine what the other girls must have been going through," Julie says.

The reality is that my other girls were used to it. We tried to be a "normal" family, do stuff like a normal family. We just could never pull it off. And after a while, we just stopped trying.

"We didn't invite people over, plan trips with other families like many people do. Family trips were a nightmare," Julie says.

"Every night was a nightmare. Fighting with her sisters, screaming at us," I say.

"Trying to keep her separate from Josie, even though they shared a bathroom," Julie says.

And when she wasn't breaking or ruining things, she was leaving messes everywhere, which was particularly hardest on Josie, our youngest daughter who even at a young age liked things orderly and neat. She and Natalie were not a good combination.

I remember thinking at the time that we should not go on that weekend trip, that we should have come up with an excuse and said we could not make it. I knew that we should have never accepted that invitation.

"We were on eggshells, waiting for something to explode. We were stressed and I am sure the other girls could sense our anxiety," I say.

"That's the real tragedy of the trip, really. It should have been a great time, particularly for the girls. Like most everything else we tried to do as a family, the one ruined it for the rest of us," Julie says.

I wish that Zoe had hit me with that rock instead of the car.

Would it have hurt?

I doubt I would have noticed.

Addiction Finds Us

"There are always articles in the paper and stories about other people and other people's children. None of that prepares you to handle it when it is your kid. There is no pamphlet for this one."

—*David*

I saw Natalie a few times during the years that she was in Florida, bouncing from halfway house to treatment program. Julie went about five years without seeing her. She doesn't remember exactly when, but I know for sure that she will never forget where it was. We drove down to some isolated spot near Boynton Beach to find her in a crack house with beds on the floor, a couple of men about my age, one who was sleeping on the floor, the other wasted off his ass and ogling at Julie when we walked through the door.

"She had a pet sheep," Julie says.

The sheep lived in the house with her and the two older dudes.

"I was sick," Julie says. "I knew what she was doing and I hated myself for leaving her there."

"We did what we had to do. We spent a fortune, all of our savings, trying to help her. We put her into that great program in Utah. And don't forget the Wilderness program for three months," I say.

We were told that Wilderness programs are where kids get "broken down." They learn to work with others and put their self-interests aside, away from the technology, social pressures, and distractions that are prevalent at home. Not our kid. No one broke her. Three months in the brutal cold of winter in the Utah mountains, about forty thousand dollars of our savings gone, and when spring broke, she was no further along. After a few months at home, she ended up hospitalized for alcohol poisoning and was accepted to an addiction program in south Florida.

"There were opportunities for her to help herself once she went off to Florida," Julie says.

"She made her choices and we had to make ours," I say.

"After the sheep house, I promised myself that I would never go to see her anywhere ever again until she was somewhere safe," Julie says.

"When do you think the addiction started?" I ask Julie. "When she tried to fill up her red gym bag with a few bottles of our alcohol?"

"No. It was long before that. And it wasn't alcohol or drugs," she says. "Natalie was addicted to manipulation, to getting her own way at any cost."

She would run away, go to people's houses, and tell them what they wanted to hear. She told anyone who would listen that we were bad parents; that we abused and mistreated her. And people believed her.

"Of course they did. She had a lot of practice. She told us things we wanted to hear for years before that," Julie says.

Good people, well-meaning people, would let her in, open their home, and welcome her to stay with them. One friend's mom even offered to give her a room and let her live at their house indefinitely. She went so far as to let Natalie pick out paint.

"Natalie stole her money," Julie says. "And her car, but just for a short trip."

She wanted to go to McDonald's. I do give her credit. My daughter never once drove a car, other than a few decidedly unsuccessful driving lessons with me in a school parking lot. She didn't take driver's education and had no license.

I still can't believe we made it through all that and kept the rest of the family sane and the household running.

Watching someone destroy herself is no easy task. Especially when it's your kid. And, I think, much harder for Julie than for me.

"Not harder. Different," Julie says.

"You spend your life working and helping kids and their families with a lot of the same behavioral and mental health issues Natalie has. They pay you for your time," I say. "But your own kid, she didn't want your help, wouldn't take it. If anything, she did all she could to fight it."

"And for you, well, you were just her dad," Julie says. "You wanted to save her, protect her, make sure she could have a good life."

I still want her to have a good life. What about the desire to save and protect? That is long gone. It took a while, but I finally came to the realization that I can't do either.

When Julie talks to her, she still tells her the same thing she told her five years ago.

"I tell her that we love her and we will be patient. We will wait for her," Julie says.

Ride in the Same Ambulance

"Parents have children. Children have problems. Agree on the treatment plan."

—Julie

More often than not it is David who needs a drink after work. The years of navigating through other people's conflict and misery weighs on him daily.

Tonight, I am the one who is in need of a bracer. I tell him to make me a cocktail.

"You sound like me. Wine?" he asks.

It's a vodka night.

While David grabs a bottle of Tito's and starts mixing me up an extra-dirty martini, I fill him in.

"I had this couple in. Sniping, fighting, blaming," I say.

"Doesn't sound good. Maybe you might want to pass my card along," he says. "What's the battle about?"

The couple is at odds over their fifteen-year-old son, Steven, who is just starting high school. The two of them are diametrically opposed to each other when it comes to how to handle him. I just started seeing him a month or so ago, right before school started. Steven is not unlike a lot of my clients, likely on the autism spectrum, with significant problems staying on task and getting along with peers. He is very bright, but he has historically underperformed academically.

"His parents wanted to meet with me, express their concerns, talk to me about strategies to help him," I say.

It is exactly what I do best. I welcome those kinds of sessions with the parents of my clients. What I didn't realize here was the level of their exasperation and even anger, not just with Steven, but also with each other.

I have a book in my office that I have read several times called *The Blessing of a Skinned Knee.*

"That was one of the hundred or so you gave me to read when our kids were little," David says.

I am not sure how many of the hundred he actually read.

"The message of the book is essentially that it is not a parent's job to make everything easy and perfect for your children," I say.

We had those issues with both of our younger girls. With Natalie, there were struggles across the board. She had trouble with academics and in social situations. She couldn't make friends. She didn't, or wouldn't, do the work she needed to do to be even moderately successful in school.

"Josie handled her struggles," David says.

Josie was diagnosed with a reading disability at a young age, probably something she got from me. I was never much of a reader in school and even now I often need to read things three or four times over before it sinks in.

"With Natalie, we tried to help, we got the supports in place. It still didn't take. She wasn't going to work with us to succeed," I say.

"Josie was different," David says.

"She was," I say.

Josie made use of those tools. She got an individualized education program (IEP) and applied those resources in order to succeed in school. She worked her butt off, frequently watching YouTube videos when she didn't understand something. If that didn't help, she would reach out for extra help from a teacher.

"We didn't leave her on her own," David says. "We did help her. We worked to get the IEP, the extra supports that came along with it."

"We did, and as parents, that was the right thing. It's one thing to help your kid, it's another to jump in and just fix it for her," I say. "What we did not do was just swoop in and do the work for her, go to the school and change her teachers or classes when something got hard for her. And, I think it is important to point out, Josie knew we were not going to do those things."

Did she experience failures? Sure she did. It was hard on the two of us to watch and let those failures play out. But today, as a college student, Josie is all the better for it. She is stronger and more self-sufficient.

Steven's parents are in a similar place. They have had a long-simmering dispute over their son and it is coming to a head right at the beginning of his high school life. Steven has always played football but now he wants to quit.

"Why does he want to quit?" David asks.

"He says it is harder; the boys are bigger. But the real reason I think is that he doesn't like getting up early or staying late for practice," I say. "He would rather be sleeping, online, or playing video games."

It doesn't end with football.

Steven doesn't like his English teacher. He says he has no friends at the school. He says the school sucks and what they are teaching him is worthless. Steven wants to go to a private school nearby where he knows a few of the students. His mom went and pulled him out of the English class and now she is fully supportive of Steven going to the private school.

"What's Dad say?" David asks.

"Dad says he needs to tough it out. He is pissed that his wife went to the school without telling him and got Steven moved into another class," I say.

His father wants Steven to stick with football and is adamantly against moving Steven to private school.

"I agree," David says.

"You're not his wife. And she doesn't agree," I say.

Mom thinks he might be more successful at the private school. She hates to see him struggling. It sounds to me like in the past whenever Steven has encountered a problem, either with a peer or in school, Mom has done whatever needs to be done to protect him, to fix or find his way out of the problem and make things as easy as she can for her son.

"She is an enabler," David says. "Dad is pissed. He thinks Mom has coddled Steven all of these years and now it is time to 'pay the piper' so to speak. His kid can't do anything on his own."

Being married to me has helped give my husband some well-tuned insights into the human condition.

Dad says Steven is lazy and weak; that he is always looking for the easy way out. He is worried that Steven will not be able to handle even the slightest of obstacles that life will inevitably present. He blames his wife for years of coddling and catering to Steven.

"Did he try to work with her before?" David asks. "During all those years that he says Mom was too easy on Steven?"

"He says he did but it looks to me like at some point he just checked out, leaving the bulk of the parenting to her. He disagreed with her, apparently expressed his opinion when Steven was younger, but ultimately just let it pass, choosing to avoid the arguing," I say.

Now he is in full "blame" mode. He told her that she created this monster, so she needs to deal with it.

Mom is just as pissed at her husband as he is at her. She says that her husband was never willing to do any of the hard parenting. He avoided the difficulties with Steven growing up, left it all to her, and she did the best she could.

"Mom doesn't think her husband has any right to be upset at her now, after all these years of abdicating his parenting role," I say.

"And you solved this entire mess during the one hour you spent with them?" David asks.

"Not so much. I did try to get them on board with the idea that what happened before is done, that Steven is their son and needs guidance and help now, from both of them. He is so used to being rescued, it will be difficult for Steven and his parents if and when they take even a slightly different approach. It will not be easy for these parents, particularly with their having been on different wavelengths for so long."

"Another one?" David asks.

My glass is empty, after all.

Letters to Our Daughter

Natalie was not yet sixteen when we sent her to a treatment program in Utah, hoping that they could help her learn how to get along with others and use her strengths to find her place in this world. It was not an easy decision, nor was it a financially sound one. The bottom line for us was simple. We could not help her, and we wanted her to get help, so we tried to find someone else who could do for her what we, as parents, were unable to do ourselves. Natalie never finished the program in Utah and instead spent the next several years running and drugging, wasting her life and almost dying on at least two or three occasions—that we know about. I am sure there were others.

In the years that have passed since she has been a real part of our family, Julie has written Natalie several letters, none of which were ever sent. At its essence, this book is one of hope. Julie and I hope that reading about what we have experienced and done ourselves will help others to think a bit more about their own relationships, and in so doing, become better parents and partners. As a result, I thought it appropriate to share a bit more of our own struggles, our own failures, and have copied here a couple of Julie's letters to our daughter just as she wrote them.

—*David*

You are Nineteen Today

It's not the way I would have envisioned things. Nineteen years ago today Dad and I went to Pittsburgh to meet you and take you as our own.

Full of hope and dreams of your future we brought you into our family. Things started off rough—allergies to everything starting when you were a baby, difficulties into toddlerhood, and years of being kicked out of places. You spent your fourteenth birthday in a psych ward, and your sixteenth birthday in a boarding school for troubled girls. I cried more times than I can count. How could I send a child that I wanted so badly off to therapeutic boarding school for someone else to parent? It was because I no longer felt like I could help you and keep you safe.

On your eighteenth birthday you were homeless, living in a tent in your friend's backyard.

Your nineteenth birthday is today and you are in a sober living community and it's the twelfth place you have lived in six months and the twentieth place you have lived in the past two years.

What I hope for you today on your nineteenth birthday isn't much. Not a new car, not a bachelor's degree, or a big role in a play. I hope you can find peace with yourself, make and keep connections with people, settle down, follow rules, keep track of your personal belongings, and plan for your future. Living in the NOW is great, but at some point, you have to look ahead.

Why am I writing you this? I can't talk to you right now. I am too hurt, afraid, and ashamed of your life and I can't change any part of it. I have chosen to keep away from you because I can't watch you live this destructive crazy life—it hurts too bad.

I hope and pray you keep yourself safe. I hope when you turn twenty I can see you and celebrate a happy productive life—the one you deserve!

Love, Mom

You Are Twenty Tomorrow

I will always be there for you.

This is what parents say to their kids. Do you know what it's like to have to turn away from your child? I bet most people don't. It's awful. My beautiful daughter will be twenty tomorrow and I have told her not to call, not to text or write. I cannot have her be a part of my life.

I know this sounds cruel but I have to do it. My daughter is an addict. She is an addict of drugs and an addict of bad behavior. Seeking out what feels good in the now, always disregarding rules and disrespecting relationships.

I can no longer be on an emotional roller-coaster hoping and praying that she does what she says she's going to do one minute, being excited for her for what looks like progress and the next minute not knowing where she is; being afraid that the most awful thing has finally happened and my little girl is dead.

I don't know what I'm supposed to do because it's her birthday and I want to wish her a happy birthday. I'm happy that she's alive at age twenty but I'm also not willing to have a relationship with her until she gets things together. It is too hard; it's too painful as a mother to watch what she's done to her life.

So, when a parent says that they will "always be there for you no matter what," it might be a lie.

I'm not quite sure what to do tomorrow on your twentieth birthday. I want to wish you a happy birthday but I can't. I can't be part of your life right now. I hope when you turn twenty-one that I can be there for you, that I can text you or call you. Maybe even hug you? I hope that I can be a part of your life again.

Happy birthday, daughter. I love you.

—Mom

To Our Other Three

"I think I have said this to my other daughters. Maybe I should say it again."

—David

Amanda, Zoe, and Jo,

We did not have the family life that we expected. We did not do all the things, go all the places, and spend all the time with the three of you that we wanted. The parties that you missed, the trips that weren't planned, the books that didn't get read before you went to sleep, that was not your fault. And no, it was not Natalie's fault. It was ours. Mom's and mine.

There were so many times that we wanted to do more but didn't because we were either too lazy or tired. Lazy because maybe on a given day, we just wanted to hang out at home instead of taking that ride over to Great Falls and walking on the Billy Goat Trail. Tired because we just couldn't bear spending another minute managing, policing, or disciplining.

I like to think that we did our best, but the fact is, looking back, we could—and should—have done better. That's a hard thing to say, particularly when parents don't get to turn the clock back or get a "do-over."

Your Mom and I know that a lot of the time it was terribly difficult growing up in our house. The yelling, the fighting, the arguing—all of it happened in your home and it happened much more than it should have. No child should ever have to put a lock on her door to keep a sibling from getting in.

We do hope that the challenges we faced as a family, and the conflicts that were much too frequent, helped to make you all stronger and mold you into the amazing independent women that the three of you have grown up to be.

I remember distinctly talking to one of you girls, I won't mention which one, after a particularly dreadful night at home trying to manage Natalie's behavior at the end of a workday. You went to your room and waited until Natalie went to bed. Only then did you come down and have dinner. I asked if you were okay. You didn't look up from your plate. You just said, "I am fine. You don't understand."

I didn't say anything.

But I did. I understood.

—Dad

Couple's Kickstarters

1. Was it difficult for you to have children? Did that cause strife between you and your partner? How did that manifest itself in your relationship and what did you do to work through it?

    _____

    _____

    _____

2. When you disagree about something your partner has done or said in terms of raising your child, do you talk to them about it or prefer to keep it to yourself?

    _____

    _____

    _____

3. Do you and your partner find it difficult maintaining consistency in setting rules for your children? If one of you says "no" does the other support that decision?

    _____

    _____

    _____

4. When you have a difference of opinion about rules or boundaries, do you discuss it with your partner away from your children or with them present?

_____

_____

_____

5. Do you and your partner have different religious beliefs? How do you handle those differences?

_____

_____

_____

6. Does your own upbringing affect how you parent or discipline your own children? Does that style differ from your partner's? Are you able to reconcile those differences so as to maintain a united front with your children?

_____

_____

_____

7. Is it difficult for you to watch your child be uncomfortable in a situation or even fail at a task? Are you and your partner able to work together in terms of when to intercede or not?

_____

_____

_____

8. Are you able to recognize when your partner needs time away from the children?

_____

_____

_____

9. Have you been the victim of a child's attempt at manipulation or triangulation? How do you and your partner work to combat that behavior?

_____

_____

_____

10. Do you worry about what other people think of your children and how that reflects on you as a parent?

_____

_____

_____

Bumping and Grinding

Julie believes I take a much too simplistic view of what it is that keeps a couple together and a relationship healthy. "In your world, so long as we are having sex regularly, everything is fine," she has said to me over and over again. And over again. Julie views me as a "one trick pony," someone whose brain dangles a very average distance down between his legs. Her way of looking at it, legs crossed and from a turquoise leather therapist's chair, is that all I need is a tug or two every week or ten days and she could drown the dog, sit around, and watch episodes of *Love It or List It* all day or spend a week culling through the women's department at Nordstrom. All would be fine, and in my world, she would still be the perfect wife.

In fairness, Julie is not entirely wrong. I mean, seriously, raise your hand if you believe that if every person in every relationship went out of their way to have regular, fun, and passionate sex with their partner, that the divorce rate would drop through the floor and I could go back to bartending or waiting tables. A lot of hands just went up. You know they did.

Just because she is right and my take on finding relationship bliss is that it is not any more difficult than turning a freshly cut key in your front door lock, it does not mean that my perspective is wrong. It isn't.

I am not suggesting that all it takes for a couple to be happy and satisfied is for them to have great sex. What I am saying though is that sex can be a gatekeeper to that happiness and satisfaction.

In my own personal life and my thirty-plus years of marriage to Julie, I can certainly say without hesitation that the chances of me having a good day, being more patient, and, frankly, just having a sunnier disposition are vastly improved if Julie and I spent a few quality minutes of heavy breathing together the night before.

We joke that ours is the "house that misery built." As a divorce lawyer, someone who earns his living primarily because other people are unhappy, that is a fair description. I have spent an unfathomable amount of time, often recorded down to tenths of an hour, talking to people who are depressed and often despondent, teary-eyed and troubled. Those people are just like you and me. They got into a relationship hoping, no, expecting a life of joy, of pleasure and fulfillment. They wouldn't be in my office, however, if that life had turned out according to plan. And one of the primary reasons those folks come to my office, sit in front of me often with a shopping bag full of bank and credit card statements in tow, is because of sex. The names and faces change, the stories vary, but one frequent commonality? Sex. No sex, not enough sex, boring sex, sex with someone else, sex with a man, sex with a woman, sex with both. Sometimes more than one of those boxes gets checked.

People and our relationships, we all differ. What works for us may not work for you. Human beings and their sex lives cannot be boiled down to a ninth-grade chemistry class. You don't put two substances into a beaker and know exactly what is going to result. The idea, though, is to understand the very central role that sex plays in most relationships. We need to understand and sometimes adjust to our partner's needs. Realize that other factors—finances, work, and children, to name a few—can all affect and, yes, be affected by sex. We need to talk to our partners about it. We need to be sensitive to his or her feelings, needs, and desires. And, in my view, we need to have more of it.

—David

It's Not a Budget Item

"Sex should be a natural thing. It doesn't hurt anyone. So why do people limit contact with their partners?"

—David

A running disagreement in our thirty-plus years of marriage has been the frequency or lack thereof, depending upon which one of us you are asking, of our having sex.

"You shouldn't withhold it," I say.

Julie of course denies withholding anything.

"I just don't want to do it as much as you do," she says.

I tell her about a new client who came to see me earlier in the day.

"He is good looking, early thirties," I say. "Dark, long hair, little scruffy beard. He is in construction. Wrangler jeans and beat up boots; had that tough guy aura about him."

"Keep going," Julie says, looking up at me over her reading glasses, adding some hot water to the bath.

I think it was the Wrangler jeans part that got her attention.

I have become much more observant over the years. After spending so much of my waking life talking to unhappy people, I notice and pay attention to most every gesture, facial expression, and change in voice intonation when they sit down in my office.

"It does sound like you are trying to use some sort of fantasy thing to get me in the mood," Julie says.

That wasn't my intention.

"Too bad. It was working," she says.

The girl is a big talker. I know she has no intention of putting her money where her mouth is, so to speak, and I fill her in on the whole back story, how he and his wife met at one of those all-inclusive resorts, hit it off immediately, and fell into a crazy sex-filled week together.

"A few days in Fantasyland," Julie says.

"Essentially, yes. They both head home after, him back here to the DC area, her to Portland, Oregon. A few weeks of texting, emailing, and phone calls and she decides to pack up and move in with him," I say.

"Not rational thought," Julie says.

This is not the first time I have heard this type of story. "So, she moves east and—shocking, I know—she gets pregnant and they decide to get married. Their daughter is now five years old, and he shows up at a divorce lawyer's office," I say.

No more Fantasyland.

"The opposite, actually," I say. She is overwhelmed and unhappy, having given up her job and friends to move to a town where she has no one."

She has no friends, no support system and Fantasyland has turned into Celibate City. She is mad at him for making her come to a town where she feels isolated, tied to a child that was not planned, and has no intention of making him happy by having sex. She is angry, so his perspective is that her withholding sex is a way to hurt him.

"Don't tell me. Let me guess," Julie says. "No sex, so he wants a divorce."

That is why people come to me, after all.

"You want to know what the Wrangler guy says to me?" I ask. "This is one of those moments over a long career that I will not forget. Word for word," I say. "He says, 'if she spent as much time on my dick as she does on Facebook, I wouldn't even be here right now.' It took all the self-control I could manage not to spit my coffee across the desk."

"I can see where you are going with this," Julie says. "Wrangler guy feels ignored. He wants his wife to pay attention to him. Since she doesn't, he wants a divorce. And as a result of all of this, I should have sex with you whenever you want."

I don't quite agree. It sounds to me as if she is using sex in a way that is unhealthy. Since she is angry with him, she knows he wants to be intimate with her, so she withholds sex. She doles it out sparingly. Like there is a shortage or an expense line on a budget that she can't go over.

"What he really should do is get her to counseling, talk about it. Do things that will help her to feel better and find ways to get her out of the house," Julie says, now out of the bath and in my closet. "If he loves her, divorce can't be the only answer."

"He does and I agree. I gave him some names of marriage counselors, talked to him about the divorce process, and sent him on his way," I say. "What are you doing in there?"

"Looking for a pair of Wranglers," Julie says.

Tussies

"It can be mundane. There are ways to fix that."

—*David*

Even I have to agree that sex sometimes is not as fun as it should be. Although we had no problem getting pregnant with our first daughter, we were unsuccessful a few years later when we were ready to add to our family.

"With Amanda, we decided we wanted to have a baby and then, boom, I was pregnant," Julie says.

It's like that old saying, if it wasn't for bad luck, I would have no luck at all.

In fairness, things got evened out later. Julie had to have surgery for endometriosis, and once she was recovered from that, we planned to start fertility treatments.

Before the fertility treatments though, the doctor put us on a sex timer. The spontaneity was gone.

"We had to do it nine times over three days or whatever," I say.

"It was awful. I dreaded the four days each month, I think it was days twelve through sixteen, that I had to let you stick it to me again and again," Julie says. "I had absolutely no interest, and spent most of the time thinking about going to the gym or what I was cooking for dinner. Whatever it took to get me through it."

Afterward, Julie had to lie in bed with her legs up in the air for a couple minutes.

"Like Bugs Bunny," she says.

It wasn't sexy. It wasn't fun.

"It was a chore," Julie says. "After the fun period, fun for you, I mean, I had to keep coming up with stuff to keep you interested."

It was the only time that she wore lingerie.

"It wasn't the only time," she says. "I just don't see the reason to spend money on something you want me to take off after two or three minutes."

"Party pooper," I say.

She is right, though. The sex timing got boring, even annoying to a certain degree.

"It got to the point that I really just wanted to be left alone. Watch TV, read, whatever. Anything other than being a pregnancy rod," I say.

That was when we looked into a video store in Wheaton, Maryland. The adult section was behind a white screen divider. Julie made me go back there. While Julie and Amanda were perusing the family section, I was hunched over, head down, doing all I could not to make eye contact with anyone.

And it wasn't easy. It was a tough decision to make. In those days, porn videos were like thirty bucks a pop. We could only afford one, and it had to be right. It wasn't easy picking between *Butt Man's European Vacation* and *A Man's Job*.

"You hit a home run with *Orgasm Alley* as I recall," Julie says.

Along with three girls' butts on the cover there was a guy with a ponytail. I knew Julie had a thing for dudes with ponytails so I grabbed the box, basically sprinted to the counter, paid in cash, and got the hell out of there with the tape jammed into a paper lunch bag.

"We got into the minivan, buckled Amanda into the back, and then you opened the bag," I say.

"I was interested," Julie says.

"You didn't stop to think that our three-year-old daughter was looking up front while you were examining the box cover to the video," I say.

She tries to convince me that she was interested in the story; wanted to see what it was all about.

"The plot, yes. It wasn't until Amanda yelled, 'Hey, I see girls' tussies' that we realized she could see the cover," I say. I thought for sure the kid was destined for a lifetime of therapy.

We got home, and put her straight to bed. Julie was out of her clothes before Amanda's door shut behind me. It was about two in the afternoon.

"Poor girl. She was so tired," Julie says.

That's Not My Finger

"People's needs and desires differ. There should be ways to adjust so that both individuals are comfortable."

–Julie

There have been a lot of times over the years when I have had to reassure David that my not wanting to have sex has nothing to do with whether I love him or not. It's just that our sex drives are different. And, pardon the pun, but it can be hard being married to someone who wants sex a lot more than I do.

"You have managed okay," David says.

He is right. I have managed, but it does get problematic.

"It always seems like it is the 'what have you done for me lately' kind of thing," I say.

David may disagree but it sure can feel that way.

"We have sex on Saturday, and then you are at me again by Tuesday, like a dog with rabies," I say.

"You are lucky it takes until Tuesday," he says.

My boy. He has such wonderful self-control.

"It's a problem for a lot of couples," David says.

It's one of his "Big Three."

David corrects me. It's really his "Big Four," my husband's oversimplification of human relationships and why they collapse. I say oversimplification, but with what he has done for more than thirty years, maybe I owe him a little more credit. Maybe not.

"A couple is happy together, they enjoy each other, are in love, have a nice family, and in all other ways have a strong, healthy relationship," David says. "One of them just has a higher sex drive. The constant requests for sex annoy their partner."

I'm thinking "demands" might be a better word than "requests," but I decide not to interrupt.

I must have made a face though.

"Okay," David says. "Let's call it pressure. The other partner is constantly feeling pressured to have sex. She is tired, worrying about other things, works all day. It can be any number of reasons. And when it is time to get in bed, rest and relax, over rolls a home version of Hugh Hefner."

"Hugh there, he constantly feels rejected because his partner keeps telling him she's too tired or not in the mood," I say.

Conversely, Mrs. Hefner feels bad about rejecting Hugh. Guilt may come first, but anger, that comes later.

"Hugh makes her feel like she is doing something wrong just because she does not, at this particular time, feel like having sex. She wants to curl up under her blankets, maybe read for a bit, and just drift off to sleep," I say.

"So, just for argument's sake, what's the big deal?" David asks. It's five or ten minutes and then she can go to sleep. Hugh is happy, no skin off her nose, and all is well. It's not like saving money, he says. I have said this before. The booty should not be on a budget."

He *has* said it before. I just don't think this issue is as neat and simple as he makes it out to be.

"Honestly, though, I don't understand why it shouldn't be easy," David says. "Hugh is not asking her to cut the grass, empty the dishwasher, mop the floors. It doesn't take long. And, by the way, it feels good and makes the person he loves feel good. What is the big deal?"

"The issue comes down to respect," I say.

Not coincidentally, David is focusing only on the needs of the partner who is looking for sex. What about the other person? Hugh's wife has a different need. She might need to relax, to be left alone, and to wind down after a long day. She's not ready to go to sleep. She needs a little time; time to herself, or even with Hugh reading in bed also. That's fine, too. But just being together, next to each other. It could be talking or maybe laughing about something one of the kids did. It just needs to be simple, quiet, and easy. It can be as basic as their laughing about an event that may have happened during the day.

"A few minutes of sex does not preclude her having any, or all, of that," David says.

"Okay, but why does, let's say she, why does she have to deal with a four- or five-inch bone prodding her in the ass first?" I ask.

"Let's call it a six-inch bone prodding in her ass," he says.

Since this is all hypothetical, I'll let him call it a six-inch bone.

"My way," David says, "they both get what they want. She takes care of him physically, and he supports her emotionally after. Everyone is happy. Winners all around."

I don't believe he and I will ever agree on this one.

All of this reminds me of the joke," I say.

"Oh no, not again," David says.

It's a funny one.

"I think it's more how you tell it," he says. "I'm laughing and you haven't even started. Go ahead."

"I suggest we do it together. You first," I say.

He starts.

"All right, all right. Can I touch your neck?"

"Yes."

"Can I touch your stomach?"

"Of course."

"Can I touch your belly button?"

"Sure. Hey, wait. That's not my belly button!"

"And that's not my finger."

Is That All There Is?

"Physical contact is important, but it doesn't always have to be about sex."

–Julie

There is absolutely no doubt that sex is an important part of any healthy relationship. For my husband, though, that seems to be it. Sex is the key, the lock, the whole kit and kaboodle. But a relationship cannot survive solely on good sex.

"I'm not so sure about that," my husband says.

I ignore him.

"Okay, sure, there is more to my being happy than sex," he says. "The things we do together, the laughs and jokes. Being out with you and having a drink, on the beach, people-watching. All that makes me happy. You are my best buddy."

I actually think I come in second to Frank, our golden retriever.

"His tail wags more than yours does," David says.

Not one for too much physical contact, I wonder if that, the touch part of a relationship, calls for more than just sex.

"You are not much of a touchy kind of person," David says.

"Is it just sex, or do you appreciate it when I touch you in other ways?" I ask.

"In all honesty, the sex piece is on top of this particular food chain," he says.

Shocking.

"But yes, there are other things," he says. "You remember last week when we were out having a drink? We were talking to Steve from up the street. At some point during the conversation, I noticed you were leaning in closely and listening to him."

Of course I was leaning in. There were a ton of people around us and it was quite loud at the bar.

"The leaning part I understood," David says. What I didn't appreciate was your hand on his shoulder while he was talking," David says.

I have no idea what he is talking about or even why it matters.

"When was the last time you put your hand around me, or on my shoulder when I was talking? When was the last time you did it at any time for that matter?" David asks.

Clearly, my placing a hand on a neighbor's shoulder for a moment or two bothered David, to whom I have been married since graduating college.

"Why didn't you say anything?" I ask.

"You know my rule," he says. "If it won't matter…"

"Don't say it."

"You were jealous because I put my hand on his shoulder?" I ask.

He says it wasn't jealousy although that is exactly what it sounds like to me.

"I knew you would think that, but you are off base. I was annoyed. Big difference," he says.

"And why were you annoyed?" I ask him.

"Because we can go days when you don't touch me," David says. "No hugs, no hand-holding, no arms around me, nothing. And certainly no hand on my shoulder when I am talking."

"It still sounds like jealousy to me," I say.

He continues to disagree, describing it as being disappointed more than anything else.

"I would like it if you touched me more, in any situation. And I am not talking about some obnoxious public display of affection," David says. "A quick hug in the morning, a slap on my butt when I am getting dressed, pretty much anything is nice. I think if you did those things with me, expressed affection that way, more frequently, the whole hand-on-Steve's-shoulder would not have affected me."

"You wouldn't have noticed it?" I ask.

"I probably would have noticed it, but it would not have bothered me like it did."

"I am so proud of you for opening up like that," I say.

I promise to do better.

"Come give me a hug," I say.

A Hitch in Your Giddyup

"Sex can cause kinks in a relationship. Find ways to loosen them."

–Julie

I had a new client recently who thinks just like my husband. He came with his wife, Beth, and immediately wanted to get right into the problems with their sex life. I barely closed the door and he was complaining about their sexual relationship being boring.

"How is it boring to him?" David asks.

"He says it's always the same routine, they don't do anything different," I say.

"What's the routine he is not happy with?"

I look at my husband. We talk about work almost every night. He rarely asks more than a question or two and usually that is only when he wants to appear interested, hoping I will appreciate his interest appropriately.

"You are really interested here, aren't you?" I ask.

"I just want to help," he says.

David is such a caring man. He really is. A philanthropist.

"Alex says that they basically do the same thing. They kiss, they touch a bit, have intercourse, and then it's over. No real passion or spice to it," I say. "Beth of course says it's all fine. They have sex regularly, two or three times a week, and they both enjoy it."

134

"Two or three times a week?" David asks.

I should not have mentioned that part.

"Beth says she enjoys it and doesn't understand the problem," I say.

"He is bored but she thinks all is well," David says. "They've got a hitch in their giddyup."

I have no idea.

"What the hell is that?" I ask.

David explains that he heard the "hitch in your giddyup" line in a western movie.

"Basically, it means that you are stuck, or slowed down, can't get moving," he says. "You or your horse, that is."

By this time, I am laughing so hard that my wine is leaking out of my nose. Thankfully, it's white and not red.

"Alex wants to bring in another girl to spice things up," I say.

"Him and the rest of us," David says. "How long have they been married?"

Alex and Beth have been married for five years. If boredom came that early in their marriage, it certainly doesn't bode well for how things will look fifteen or twenty years down the road, assuming they get that far.

"Has Beth signed up for the threesome?" David asks.

"Not at all. She is not comfortable with it. She thinks that bringing a third person into their sex life will upset what they have together," I say.

Although Beth has no sexual fantasy that would push her toward inviting another participant into their bedroom, she is primarily worried about how it will affect the bonds she and Alex share, the friendship aspect of their relationship.

"Beth thinks it's better to have a vanilla sex life, if that's what he thinks it is, than to risk ruining everything else. For her, their sex life is fine, it's fulfilling, it's all she needs," I say.

For his part, Alex is not even the slightest bit worried about what will happen after he fulfills this fantasy thing of his.

"He is all in for it. So, they came to me to discuss the ramifications, the possible consequences of doing what Alex wants and trying the threesome idea," I say.

"I can think of one unpleasant consequence, for Alex anyway," David says. "The whole thing will last about forty seconds."

"Very funny, but try to move your thinking up to your brain for a minute," I say. "Maybe Alex will like her more?"

"And what if Beth likes her more?" David asks; that mind of his is working overtime at this point.

There are a lot of potential potholes here. Will one of them get jealous? Do they only get together when all three are available? What are the rules?

I try not to go sideways on this. It's not my job as the therapist to say what is right or wrong. I am trying to work with the two of them to see how it is what they do, or don't do, might impact other areas of their relationship. And on top of that, I tried to help them find other ways to get to a place more exciting and sexier for Alex that Beth still finds comfortable.

"That's a lot to do in an hour," David says.

We won't get it all done in an hour. With Beth, I had Alex reiterate how much he loves her, appreciates her, and values their relationship. Without blaming or seeming angry, he asked her to be a little more playful or experiment more when it comes to sex.

"We talked about Alex coming up with other ideas that might also be just as fun or exciting, but that did not involve someone else so as to avoid some of Beth's concerns," I say. "Like watching sexy movies or one of them reading something hot from a book to the other. Maybe Beth dressing up, some playacting, or using sex toys."

"How did it all go over?" David asks.

The session got them both thinking about what the other feels and wants from their relationship and that there doesn't need to be a black-and-white kind of answer. Instead, maybe there can be a resolution that they both can be comfortable with.

"I have a question," David says. "You ever heard the term 'practice what you preach'?"

"Giddyup and get out of here, mister," I say.

To Porn or Not to Porn

"It's a lot more than just squirreling away your Dad's center-fold or trying to see through the plastic magazine wrapping at the 7–11."

—*David*

Can pornography be a healthy piece of a couple's sexual relationship? That is an issue that has come up more and more frequently for me in my law practice. With the Internet having become almost another appendage, like an arm or leg, the use of pornography is often a mine-field for conflict between couples.

"I know where this conversation is going," Julie says. "Every time we talk about pornography, you want to take my clothes off."

"To be clear," I say, "I want your clothes off all the time. It doesn't matter what we are talking about."

She puts her hand up in the air like a traffic cop, making it clear that I am to stay put on my side of the room.

My own sense is that assuming both partners are open to it, por-nography can be part of a healthy sexual relationship. In the world of divorce, however, it can also be the root of a wide swath of emotions, many of them not positive. When it comes to their partner's use or desired use of pornography, my clients have expressed anger, disap-pointment, resentment, and even jealousy.

"That's surprising. I would have thought you were firmly in the good column," Julie says, pun intended.

Pornography can have a positive effect on a relationship particularly when one or both partners travel as part of his or her job.

"How so?" Julie asks.

"Say you are married, committed to your spouse," I say.

"You mean you are a male, committed to a female," Julie says. "Its men who go out and cheat more than women, right?"

"A little sexist, don't you think?" I ask.

In my experience, particularly over the last ten years or so, I have found that assumption to be way off base. I haven't taken a poll or kept a diary, but from the desk I sit behind, women stray just as much as men.

"Anyway, yes, say it's a male who is away on a business trip. He travels a lot. Meets, has dinners with coworkers, customers, a lot of whom are women," I say. "While he doesn't have motive, he does have opportunity."

I apologize for the lawyer-speak.

"He is not inclined to cheat, no, but he does have that thing swinging between his legs that can cause trouble, get in the way sometimes," I say. "But now, with pornography immediately at his fingertips, five minutes on his iPad or iPhone and the edge is off, the urge should be gone. For a few hours at least."

"People actually watch porn on their phones? On that little screen?" Julie asks.

"There is no screen too small to see a naked woman," I say.

"Let's stay away from talking about size. Bigger is always better, baby," she reminds me, a middle-aged male of no more than average size.

Julie shifts us back to the therapist's couch.

"I do think porn can be part of a good healthy sexual relationship as well, assuming both partners consent and enjoy it," she says. "I don't mean that it should be all a couple does, but to get folks in the mood, maybe help them explore new things, new positions, that kind of thing. It can add spice to a sexual relationship."

"I agree completely," I say. "Can I come over now?"

She puts the hand back up.

"Don't forget how watching a few minutes of porn helped when we wanted to get pregnant."

"I remember. Whenever I was ovulating. Night after night after night. Even you had a hard time getting in the mood," she says.

"I wouldn't go quite that far. But I agree, it helped loosen you up a little bit," I say. "Grease the wheels, so to speak."

Julie wants to know the other, less positive effects of pornography on divorcing couples. As anyone who grew up in the seventies, eighties, or before can confirm, both access to pornography and the nature of its content have changed dramatically over the years. I have seen how pornography can cause enormous pressure not only on a couple's sexual relationship but also stress us from a parenting perspective.

"There can be a lot of problems. Let's start with kids," I say. "When I was young, the only way to see a woman naked was to heist a copy of someone's father's Playboy and hide it in the basement. And people having sex? No way you could see that."

"Maybe that's why so many boys were bad at it back then," Julie says.

Information I didn't really need, by the way.

"I wasn't one of them," I say. "Now, of course, any kid with a phone can watch porn, any kind of porn. Kids look at that stuff and think that's how sex is always supposed to be."

"Eyes rolling, moaning uncontrollably, loud, panting, all of that," Julie says.

"And a lot more. Threesomes, anal, squirting, you name it," I say.

I get the expected response.

"Gross," Julie says.

"Okay, but you work with teenagers," I say. "Their hormones are raging; they are impulsive and naive. Stupid."

"All true," Julie says. "What they don't see is that sex, healthy sex, should be about a relationship, love, a connection with your partner."

I'm not entirely sold on the sex has to equal love thing, but I let it pass.

"I know what you are thinking," she says. "And of course, it doesn't always have to be about love, but again the people should be mature, adult enough to handle it."

I am certainly cognizant of the myriad of problems created in the brain of a young person whose primary sexual education has come from the Internet. Even inside an adult relationship, however, porn can cause problems. I have seen folks in my office whose spouses think their sex lives should mirror what they see in five-minute video clips online. I had a client not too long ago who told me she liked sex, had no problem with having it as frequently as her husband wanted. More even.

"Must have sounded to you like the perfect woman," Julie says.

"Hey, I don't judge. But, yeah, she did," I say.

"The problem for her wasn't the sex part of it," I say. "It was all she had to do in order to actually have sex with her husband. She had to be dressed one way or the other, a candy striper one night, a librarian the next. He liked to record everything, so they had to stop, make sure the camera angles were just right. It ruined it for her. She couldn't just enjoy sex with her husband. She had to do it the way he wanted her to, the way he saw it in the porn he watched."

"That's unhealthy," Julie says.

It is also unrealistic.

"That's one reason it's unhealthy," Julie says. "I agree with you that partners adding pornography to their sex lives, as we already talked about, is fine, it seems to me. It just can't take over and be the main thrust of their sex lives."

Thrust. I'm not sure if she intended that one.

"You can't live your life in a porn video, is that what you mean?" I ask. She agrees.

I don't think I can keep this up. "Can I come over now?" I ask.

"All right already," she says. "And bring your iPad."

Is There Even Such a Thing?

"Yes, it is possible to have bad sex."

—David

I was on a local cable television show about a year ago, serving on a panel that was talking about sex and its impact on relationships. I was not quite sure what a divorce lawyer was doing there, behind a contemporary table top desk and pinched in between a sex therapist and the CEO of a large sex toy distribution company. My counterparts were both women, both professionals, and each obviously came to the table with some expertise in the world of sex. Me, I just like it.

During the course of the roundtable discussion, our host began talking with the sex therapist about how she deals with couples where one of the partners is critical of his or her partner's sexual skills. At one point, my Dr. Ruth-like friend made a comment about a client having made mention of his wife giving "a bad blowjob." That of course posed the million-dollar question that I did not hesitate to ask: "Is there really such a thing as a bad blowjob?"

I was serious. I personally have never experienced anything bad about a blowjob. I have a lot of friends. Male friends. Many have bragged about getting one, described where they got one, what the girl was wearing when she gave one, but never—not once—have I heard anyone say they got a bad one.

"I can't speak to a bad blowjob," Julie says, "but certainly people are often unhappy with the quality of their sex lives."

I am not sure she gets it. I am not talking about erectile problems, or other medically or psychologically related sexual dysfunction or illness.

"For some women, intercourse can be painful. And when that happens, sex isn't good, believe me," Julie says. "I have a client who told her husband, plain and simple, and with me right there, that she did not enjoy sex with him. There was no foreplay, nothing sensual when they had sex. He was too rushed, dry humping her for a while, groping her breasts, and then (according to her, anyway) just stuck it in when he was ready. She never was, and it hurt."

"He sounds like a real romantic," I say. "Dry humping? Isn't that for teenagers in a car or on mom's couch while an old *Friends* episode is on?"

"It doesn't have to be. Some adult couples might find it to be a turn on. Makes them feel like they are seventeen again," Julie says.

I had not thought of that.

"And some men, even adult men who have been having sex for years, they just don't understand the female anatomy, where things are, what needs to be rubbed or touched or whatever," Julie says. "And although I am not a man, I have had male clients who tell me that their sex lives are not as fun or exciting as they want them to be."

"These are men in relationships, I assume. I mean, if you are talking about some guy who spends his free time by himself toggling back and forth between Netflix and Pornhub, I would not expect he would have too exciting of a sex life," I say.

"Yes. Men whose wives basically roll over, do what they feel they have to, then go to sleep or back to reading a book," Julie says.

If in fact both genders experience "bad sex" with their partner, it does not seem like the fix should be all that difficult to make.

"Good sex, or bad, is a sensory thing and not just what we feel in our genitals," Julie says. "It's what we see, hear, taste, and feel. A striptease or some other dress up play, a little sexy music, strip poker, blindfolds or sex toys, whatever people feel okay with that gets them excited and in the mood is all good."

"Okay, but a bad blowjob? I ask.

"Not from me," she says.

I Don't Need Another Job

"You don't want your partner to feel as if sex is a responsibility. We all have enough of those."

–Julie

There are nights when I get in bed and literally cross my fingers hoping I don't get the poke. This is one of those nights. It's Tuesday, I drove back and forth to Silver Spring, almost two hours in the car in traffic, saw clients all day with no break and another two when I got home. I had to pay our bills, and since it's the first of the month, send out bills to my clients. Jo has an issue with something at school she needs me to help with. I don't need DB looking to give me another job to do before I go to sleep.

"Please don't ask me tonight," I say.

"I had no intention of asking you for anything," David says, "And even if I did, seriously, it's not like I would be asking you to go out and rake the leaves."

"No more jobs today is all I mean," I say.

"Sex with me is a job?" he asks.

The truth is that it does feel that way sometimes.

"I know you are going to get all pissy over this," I say, "but there are times when it's just enough. I can't do it. I don't want to do it."

"I do understand that. Happens with me too," he says.

Sure it does. Once probably back in 2004 when he had the flu.

"Honestly, though, I don't think you understand. Sex can create a tussle between couples, cause arguments, and create dissension in a relationship that frequently converts into longer lasting conflict.

"If you would just do it when I ask, we wouldn't argue," David says.

"If a partner is pressured to have sex, feels like she has to, not only does it take away from what happens between her and her partner on that particular occasion, but also has a longer, more insidious effect on their relationship," I say.

It starts I think with feelings of being pressured, possibly disrespected.

"How is she being disrespected when her partner wants to enjoy being with her?" David asks.

"Because it isn't what she wants at that particular moment and her partner sighs or moans, maybe makes some sort of sarcastic or 'poor me' kind of remark," I say. "She feels badly and decides it is just easier to give him the go-ahead. 'Sure, let's go' she says when really 'I can't wait to get it over with' is what she is thinking."

"And you are saying that there is some sort of deleterious effect on the relationship that continues after this enormous sacrifice?" he asks.

That is exactly what I am saying. She was pressured into doing what she didn't want to do. She is angry and resentful but her husband of course is completely oblivious. Now happy and pleased, he has a snack, a beer, watches some TV, and conks out.

"What he doesn't realize is that his five minutes, or less, of pleasure now has led to a much lengthier period of bad feelings for the person on the other side of the bed," I say.

"So, what should he have done when she made it clear to him that she was not interested?" David asks. "Somehow all of these 'bad feelings' are his fault? Is that what you are saying?"

As much as I may hate to admit it, David is making a good point.

"I think, to be fair," I say, "responsibility to avoid this type of thing rests on both of their shoulders. Rather than tell him the way it made her feel in a somewhat unpleasant tone..."

"Nasty, you mean," David says.

"However you want to couch it, she should tell him how she feels in a different, more positive kind of way," I say. "Something like 'There is nothing I would rather do than fool around with you but I am just exhausted. Can we plan on tomorrow? Trust me, I will have a lot more energy then.' Something along those lines."

"Works for me," David says.

I knew it would.

Two Minutes and a Tissue

"Sometimes it's just easier to lend a hand."

–Julie

"Sexy time tonight?" David asks me.

It's Wednesday.

"Hump day," he says.

Every day is hump day to him.

This has been a cause for debate since Day One. Our sex drives are different. I just don't want it as much as he does.

"No problem with your sex drive before we got married," David says.

"I needed to hook you in," I say.

It worked.

The good news is that, after years of being twisted up over this, I seem to have solved the problem. I like to call it the "complimentary hand job." It's my gift to David that keeps on giving.

"It's like a free drink at the blackjack table," David says. "On the house. I am forever grateful, but how did you come up with it?"

Not the hand job. Someone else thought of that. The "complimentary" part is all my idea.

It is the end of a long day with work and cooking and clients and cleanup. I had my bath and I am ready to go to sleep. I hop into bed and David is on his side, staring at me like he often does, looking like he hasn't had a meal in days. And I am a porterhouse steak, cooked "Pittsburgh style" just the way he likes it. He strokes my hair, maybe kisses my cheek. I smile because I have to, but keep my eyes closed. What I am thinking, hoping, really, is that he will roll over the other way and go to sleep. Leave me the hell alone.

"I don't give in that easy," David says.

Then he starts telling me how pretty I am and wedges a hand between my legs.

"That's one of my best moves," he says.

"No comment. It's definitely your silent plea for some action. And, sorry, but I am definitely not in the mood," I say.

In years past, when we were first married, the kids were younger, I would have kept my eyes shut, given him a quick kiss, told him to sleep well, rolled over the other way, and that would have been that.

"You did that many times," David says.

And then he would get pissed, make a grunt or a grumble of something unintelligible, and turn on his Kindle. What was worse was that it often carried into the next day.

"You are such a pain in the ass," I say.

I had not done anything wrong. I was tired and wanted to sleep. But Mr. Selfish Boner-Head made me feel guilty, like I was shortchanging him somehow. It was irritating beyond belief. I was just tired of feeling like I had to have sex. Just like I had to cook, I had to clean, I had to do the laundry. I was just tired of having to do things.

"So, what changed?" he asks.

"I figured you out," I say. "Kind of a sexual satisfaction epiphany. I came to realize that keeping you happy doesn't really take too much effort and very little time. Two minutes, to be exact. Give or take."

"You make me sound simple," David says.

He is simple. It's easy. I pull up my nightgown, show him a little something, talk dirty, whatever it takes.

"Don't stop now," he says.

"Say please," I tell him.

He says "please."

"I whisper, rub up against you, maybe moan like I'm auditioning for a sex hotline or porn movie. tell you how big you are. How much I need that big hard thing of yours."

In other words, I lie.

"Don't stop now," he repeats.

"I run my hand inside of your thigh, grab what needs to be grabbed," I say.

"How about you keep it up and come on over here," David says.

"And what?"

"And I promise I won't bother you tonight," he says.

"Sure, big man," I say. "Go grab a tissue."

Simple.

Couple's Kickstarters

1. Do you and your partner talk about your sexual relationship? Things that he or she does that you enjoy doing together?

   _____

   _____

   _____

2. Have you used sex as a bargaining chip in your relationship? Why?

   _____

   _____

   _____

3. Do you find sex to be a chore? Why do you feel that way? Is it something you feel that you have to do to keep your partner happy? Have you two discussed these feelings?

   _____

   _____

   _____

4. Have you and your partner worked to improve the quality of your sexual relationship? What strategies or things have you tried? Were they helpful? Did you both enjoy them?

_____

_____

_____

5. Do you communicate to your partner, either verbally or with physical touch, that you find him or her to be attractive?

_____

_____

_____

6. Do you and your partner have differing sexual desires or sex drives? Have you been able to reconcile those differences? If so, how?

_____

_____

_____

7. Do either of you feel unfulfilled in your sexual relationship? Have you discussed those feelings?

_____

_____

_____

8. Has your partner asked that you engage in sexual activities that you did not want to do or were not comfortable with? Did that cause conflict? How have you resolved that conflict?

_____

_____

_____

9. Do you feel you need an emotional connection in order to have sex with your partner?

_____

_____

_____

THE FIFTH CORE

It's a Balancing Act

What is it that keeps couples together? Communicating with each other, being aware of each other, rowing in the same boat? Thousands of books have been written, speeches given, seminars taken, all to try to find out the same thing. In my practice, I tell people to start with the Cowardly Lion's speech from *The Wizard of Oz*:

What makes a king out of a slave? Courage.

What makes the flag on the mast to wave? Courage.

What makes the elephant charge his tusk in the misty mist or the dusky dusk?

What makes the muskrat guard his musk? Courage.

What makes the Sphinx the Seventh Wonder? Courage.

What makes the dawn come up like THUNDER? Courage.

What makes the Hottentot so hot?

What puts the "ape" in ape-ricot?

Whatta they got that I ain't got?

All of us have probably seen the movie. We know exactly what the lion ain't got. And if I had a little more creativity, I would come up with a punchy little speech of my own for couples searching for a similar, simple, and easy one-word answer. So, what would it be? What do they got that you two ain't got? Balance.

I am not the first mental health professional or couples' counselor to preach the benefits of balance in a relationship. But what exactly does maintaining balance look like in the construct of a couple's relationship?

Sometimes when we are driving on the highway, we come up behind a small car that has a "wide load" sign on the back. That car is trailing some humongous vehicle that is swaying back and forth, taking up more than one lane of traffic. The small escort car is tasked with keeping the vehicle in front and its cargo safe from the various dangers on the road. If the escort car switches lanes, falls behind, or moves ahead, the truck carrying the wide load is at risk of a collision, slipping off the road, losing its way, and damaging all that it is transporting.

Instances often come up during the course of relationships where one person is dealing with something that causes her to be more needy, more dependent on her partner. It could be the death of a parent, a conflict at work or loss of a job, a medical or mental health worry, an out of control child. That person's attitude, her outlook, everything she does, is being affected and weighed down by something that she is having trouble managing. She is the wide load and she needs help, protection, and guidance. It is incumbent upon her partner to be that escort car, to help her stay in her lane until she gets through the situation and can do so herself. Couples in a committed relationship inherently understand this concept. Today I might be the wide load; tomorrow it could be my turn in the escort car.

For many years, David and I had a very difficult and trying time raising our third daughter. Not a day went by without her screaming at or arguing with us or one of her sisters. She was frustrating, maddening, and impossibly difficult. On an almost daily basis, one of us became the wide load. We couldn't do it anymore. We each understood when the other became the wide load and would generally do a good job of shifting into the escort car role. David would clean the kitchen and give baths while I went for a run or visited with my girlfriend across the street. Balance. I would take the kids out so he could turn his music up and have a beer. Balance.

Being able to toggle between the wide load and the escort car is but one example of balance in a relationship. Albert Einstein said that in order to keep your balance, you have to keep moving, and I am certainly in no position to argue with him. In a balanced relationship, a couple spends quality time together, but each person has interests and activities that are separate; they can be best friends, but still maintain their other relationships; they learn to expect things from their partner, but not take anything for granted. A balanced relationship calls for the two people to communicate, talk, and even disagree with each other, but at the same time, know when to just wait and be quiet.

Balance is not a mathematical formula. What constitutes balance in my relationship may look quite different than what it does in yours. Strive and do what you can to find it. When you do, you too will "have got what some others have got."

—Julie

Costco

"A lot of good sense can be found in the aisles of big box stores."

—Julie

I was at Costco yesterday. I absolutely love it there. David hates all big box stores—Walmart, Home Depot, and Costco are among them.

"There's something fucked up about being able to buy orange juice and a sixty-five-inch flat screen in the same aisle," David says.

I don't think the juice and electronics are in the same aisle.

"Same difference," he says. "Stop for a taster of a new kind of Italian bratwurst and then go five feet away to get your eyes examined and buy a new pair of glasses. It's a ridiculous bait-and-switch thing they have going there."

I am not following.

"It happens every time you go," he says. "You have a list of groceries to get and you come back with a winter coat, two sweaters, and a new lamp."

"I did get the groceries, too," I say.

It was right before the holidays when I was there last and the place was mobbed. I thought I had made it through my list and gotten all that I needed when I was waiting in line to check out.

"Needed, right," David says.

It was a vest, not a coat, and it was turquoise! I had to have it.

I waited a good while but when it was my turn to start checking out, I realized that I forgot to get face wipes for the girls. I already had put some of my stuff on the conveyor but I dashed off, heading across the store for the face wipes with a long line of unhappy people and their carts waiting behind me.

"And when I got back, all those people were craning their necks, glaring at me. Like I was a serial killer or something," I say.

I knew they would be pissed, I did. But I needed those face wipes. And when I pinched myself back past all of them, my first thought was to just say I was sorry, that I didn't realize it would take me so long, and thought I would make it back in time to keep the line moving.

"Lots of luck with that one," David says.

"Right. So, I didn't say that," I say. "I blamed myself one hundred percent. I looked each of them straight in the eye and apologized for wasting their time waiting for me. I offered no excuses; just said it was my fault and owned up to it."

Just a small tweak of my response led to a completely different reaction from the other customers. Instead of leaning on some excuse like "I didn't know it would take me that long," I fell on the sword, as David likes to say. I took the blame completely and in doing so I defused their anger. My mistake wasted their valuable time. I was selfish. It was a purposeful act on my part and I fessed up.

"There was nothing they could say. I paid, got my stuff, and left," I say.

As I was driving home, it hit me that all of us could learn a little about what just happened to me at Costco. Too many people in relationships make excuses. Pass the blame. I forgot. I had to work late. I was too tired.

I am convinced that there would be a lot less antagonism between couples if people just came clean and took the blame. Do what I did at Costco. Apologize. Admit to making a mistake. Tell your husband you did it and you are sorry. That's it. It's hard to argue, be mean, or angry at someone who came clean about being wrong, making a mistake, and apologizing for it.

"Did you get any of that bratwurst?" David asks.

As a matter of fact, I did. And a new TV, too.

Cussing to Kissing

"Slow and steady can win the race. But is it too boring?"

–Julie

Not a day goes by that I don't recognize how lucky the two of us are. I hear it from David every day when he comes home from work. Not too many couples make it past thirty years.

"Seventeen of the happiest years of my life," he says.

It's one of his favorite lines.

"Always gets a laugh," he says.

It does.

I see a lot of couples in my practice whose relationships always seems to be on a pendulum, like one of those carnival rides.

"It's called The CraZanity ride," David says. "People are strapped into a huge pendulum machine that swings from one side to the other. At the top of one, you are upside down, and at the top of the other, you are looking straight down from fifty feet up."

I'm not intimating that we have not experienced our share of highs and lows, but one of the positive components to our relationship is that we don't really experience them at extreme levels.

"I mean we don't swing too far back and forth between 'gaga' kind of love one day, hating each other the next," I say.

"There's nothing wrong with the gaga kind of love, I don't think. I wouldn't mind being gaga'd over once in a while," David says.

I ignore his mediocre attempt at self-pity.

In my view, those couples that are on a more even keel, not the ones that are overly infatuated one day and ready to strangle each other the next, those are the couples that get along better in the long run.

"I really do think that one of the reasons we have stayed together is that we are pretty consistent," I say. "You aren't calling me a bitch one day, then rubbing my feet the next."

"I might call you a name, but it would be under my breath. And rub your feet? Anytime," he says.

I put my feet on his lap.

"Sure. I do agree that some relationships are successful, like ours, where there are not a lot of big swings. Bumps, arguments, blips, sure. But overall things are 'steady as they go,' so to speak," David says.

Others can be successful too, but they take a different tact. They are more combustible.

For those couples, big swings are the norm. They are a part of the fabric of their relationship. It's okay to yell, to scream, and get it out. Be angry for a period of time.

"And then they swing back to infatuation. Big, fat, wet kisses. Loud and sloppy, just the way you like it," David says. "Makeup sex."

It sounds exhausting.

"For some people, though, tumult is the norm," David says. "They are used to it, comfortable with it. They thrive on it."

I just don't see how that kind of inconsistency, here to there, "ping-pongy" kind of relationship can be healthy.

"I have many people who come in for an initial consult with me," David says. "We have an hour or two meeting in my office when I ask a lot of questions and get a good bit of background about the relationship. I try to answer their questions, usually about process, what they should do in the event that they decide to separate, what happens to kids and money, the whole gamut."

And even though they are in a divorce lawyer's office, they are not necessarily looking to get divorced.

"Oftentimes the person is just looking to 'explore his options,'" David says. "Maybe he is in a down period, been unhappy for a few weeks. For some people, believe it or not, it was just a bad weekend. He wants to know, hypothetically, what he is 'in for,' what could happen if the two of them split up. And I can tell you that some of those folks have quiet, even relationships, as you called it, while others swing more on that pendulum."

"So, what happens with those people? The ones who come to 'explore their options?'" I ask.

"Some of them go home, I guess, and figure things out. Others call me back and hire me," he says.

The therapist in me still believes that it is easier for a consistent, calmer type of relationship to survive.

"For some people, calm and even-keeled is mundane and too vanilla. It's just like in your work with people. Some thrive in high-pressure environments or like conflict; others shy away from those kinds of things. Successes can be found either way," David says.

"I guess. But over the long haul, I think relationships like ours have a better chance of success," I say. "Slow and steady wins the race, it seems to me."

But is it boring?

Assbook

"Social media sites are plastered with photos of family vacations, pronouncements of pride in children, and life's successes. Shouldn't there be a place for the other stuff?"

—David

Facebook is Julie's primary connection to what is going on in the world. She doesn't read the paper, rarely watches the news, and to someone whose daily routine for the last forty or so years has included reading the *Washington Post* from cover to cover, I find it a little unnerving. Literally, before she even gets out of bed in the morning, Julie is on her phone, zipping through her Facebook feed.

"I'm not sure why it bothers you," she says. "I like to see what is going on with people. Look at all the birthdays today. Cheryl is headed to the Bahamas. The Bradys' kid just got into Virginia Tech."

Big news.

"It's nice. People have so many things going on. I like to see what they are doing. It's a way to stay in touch," she says.

I'm thinking that maybe she should brush her teeth and get dressed first.

"I think it is a bit strange that the first thing you think to do after your beauty sleep is to grab your phone and check out the latest Facebook posts," I say.

"I do need my beauty sleep. Eight hours or I'm not right. Nine is even better," she says. "And you read the paper when you go downstairs."

"Lots of differences there," I say. "I get up and get dressed first. I even brush my teeth. I walk the dogs, make some breakfast. Coffee if it's a Sunday. Then, I read the paper. And the paper gives you news, what is going on in the world. Important things to know and be aware of."

"Let's not get too high-and-mighty about things, dude," Julie says. "You start with the Sports page."

"It's college basketball season. The Terps open in a couple of days."

I don't care what she says. There is simply no comparison between the start to a college basketball season as opposed to a picture of something Ken ate last night that was "dee-lish," Karen's pledging her love to her BFF, or one of those annoying "look at my feet, I'm at the beach" photos. Please.

"That's why it's called a newspaper. It's news," I say.

"So is Facebook. It's all news. News about where people went on a vacation, who they had dinner with, their son's scholarship, birthday parties. Things like that," she says. "And unlike the paper, its usually good news."

"But people want everyone to only know the good stuff; the trips, the graduations, and the awards. There is not too much about the rest of life. I can't say I've ever seen a post like 'My husband cheated on me,' 'Just got divorced,' 'Lost my kids in a custody battle.' That sort of thing," I say.

Julie starts laughing in her eleventh-grade high school girl way that is crazy contagious. And cute.

"Something like 'I had diarrhea this morning,' or 'My hair is falling out.' That would be great," she says.

Now she is catching on. Think of the endless entertainment if we could do an upside-down Facebook?

"We'd call it Assbook," I say.

There was an episode of *Seinfeld* that was centered on "Bizarro Jerry." Elaine met a guy; a new friend who looked just like Jerry, but unlike Jerry, this fellow was courteous and thoughtful. He was Jerry's exact opposite. Assbook would be the Bizarro Facebook.

"So, all the bad stuff that happens to people, that's what goes on your Assbook page," Julie says.

That's the ticket. All the bad shit that people don't like to talk about.

"Instead of a profile photo, someone could have a picture of their daughter's DUI citation," I say.

"You could be on to something," Julie says. "Look, DB! Mary's daughter ran away."

"And Fred saw her picture is on a milk carton," I say.

"And John is bipolar and off his meds," Julie says.

"He burnt down the house," I say.

"Tom fucked his secretary and Sarah has it on tape," Julie says.

I am more certain than ever that we are both going to hell. But first I need to read the paper. And Julie needs to brush her teeth.

More or Less

"It is not unusual to feel as if your relationship is missing something or has too much of something else."

–Julie

When I work with couples, I find it is often easy to use other lifestyle constructs in challenging them to improve their relationship. For example, when someone wants to lose weight, they eat less, exercise more, or both. Similarly, if we want to save money, it's easy, we need to spend less or make more. The concepts are mirrored in a healthy relationship. More and less. What does a good relationship need more of? Or could do with less of?

"More sex, less sleep," David says. That is a shocking response from him to be sure.

"More knowledge, less wondering," I say.

It is important for the two people in a relationship to know what to expect, to know what is going on with their partner. A relationship is hampered when one or both individuals are unsure of things, where they stand, that kind of thing. That leads to insecurity in a relationship.

"I see that all the time," David says. "A woman comes to see me, I ask the usual set of questions, just to give me a background, a baseline of things so that I can start to understand why she is in a divorce lawyer's office. I might ask her if her husband travels for work. She tells me yes, so I ask her how frequently. In response I hear something like:

'I never really know, sometimes it's twice a month, sometimes it's three times. Depends.' 'Depends on what?' I ask. She doesn't know. Why does he need to travel for work? Does he have customers or clients out of town that he needs to visit? And where does he go? Don't know and not sure. That not knowing, when he will go next, where he will go, it creates anxiety."

"And mistrust," I say. "The wondering, the not being sure about what your partner is doing, where he is doing it, it saps energy from a person and can be damaging and even toxic to a relationship."

"For me, I'd like us to talk more in the morning and have you read the paper a little less," I say.

"I do both at the same time," David says. "Reading the paper doesn't keep me from talking to you."

He can, unless he is reading about a basketball game from the night before. Then he shushes me.

"That is not the same as two people having dinner together at the same table with one of them being silent while the other wants to talk, even if it's about nothing particularly important or even interesting," David says.

"Like my latest purchase at Gypsy Teal?" I say.

"Could be that," David says. "You are excited; you want to tell me about a new sweater. Forget of course it's the third one you got from there in the last month or so. You want to tell me who you ran into and talked to in the store, how the sweater is so soft, whatever. Who cares? I don't. But you want to tell me and that's what really matters."

"And instead of being interested, or even faking it, you keep reading," I say.

"Maybe I give you a head nod or something, but that's about it," David says. "This is all hypothetical of course."

"Hypothetical, sure," I say. "But yes, it would make me feel bad. Angry."

His silence or something close to it tells me essentially to be quiet, that he is not interested.

This is not exactly rocket science. Pay attention to your partner. Appear interested, even if they are not talking about the most thrilling topic in the world.

Another frequent problem occurs when people don't say what they feel or what is on their mind and instead keep whatever it is bottled up inside.

"More saying what you feel, less keeping it inside. Less repressing," David says.

I have a couple that comes to see me. They moved here a few months back from a big house out west somewhere. Two kids in school and an infant, and there was a ton to unpack. Wife is home during the day, kids go to school, and Husband goes to work early, is home around dinnertime, often after. When he gets home, nothing has been unpacked, except of course whatever he unpacked the night before.

"After working all day?" David asks.

That is exactly right. He comes in, looks at the dining room, the boxes still stacked from floor to ceiling.

"What does he say when he gets home?" David asks.

That's the problem. He doesn't say anything. He eats his dinner, thinks to himself how lazy she is, how she has all day around the house and does nothing.

"But she's not doing nothing," David says.

"Of course she's not," I say. "She is getting the kids off to school, taking care of the baby, going to the grocery store, making dinner, and doing the laundry. And more."

Husband finishes his dinner, drops his dishes into the sink, rolls up his sleeves, and starts unpacking. He is fuming. And this goes on night after night until he eventually says something, but "says" is the wrong word. He doesn't "say" anything. He yells, screams, goes into a tirade about her being worthless, that he has to do everything and is tired of working his ass off to support the family, being gone for twelve hours a day, only to come home and have to unpack boxes again.

"And what does she do?" David asks.

"You know what she does," I say. "She screams back, she is taking care of his children, she had to take the baby to the doctor, and he wouldn't nap. Calls him ungrateful, an asshole. 'What about the dinner that is right in front of you? How do you think it got there?' She slams some silverware, tells him to fuck himself or some other such thing, and storms upstairs, a slammed door serving as the exclamation point."

"All in front of the kids," David says.

"You got it. When all it would have taken is his saying something., nicely, a few days earlier," I say.

So, what should Husband have said? What should he have done? For one thing, he should have taken a more positive approach.

"Husband could have told her that he understood there was a lot of unpacking to do and if maybe she could get to one box during the day while he is gone, he will do a couple when he gets home," I say. "Then they are in it together, so when he comes home and has to unpack a bit, there is a little less for him to do."

"And Husband knows Wife has made an effort, helped out while he was out at the office all day," David says. "Explosion, fighting, and anger averted, right?"

More or less.

The Minivan

"Pay attention to the little things that your partner says or needs. Doing so might avoid a controversy later."

—David

Julie has a habit of making conversation at two particular times each day, both of which are when I am not really up for talking. The first is in the morning when I am reading the paper or trying to get myself together and head off to the office. The second occurs at night when she is in her tub and I am just ready to hop into bed, read for a few, and go to sleep.

"I was talking about a minivan," she says.

We haven't had a minivan in twenty years.

"A client's minivan," she says.

"Your client has a minivan," I say, stopping in my tracks on the way to bed. "Sorry I missed it." Not really.

"This woman is forty-three. She told me about going to the grocery store, and when she was loading her groceries in the back of the van, she noticed how dirty it was," Julie says.

Minivans mean lots of kids. Lots of kids mean lots of mess.

"There were juice boxes, wrappers, and crumbs everywhere," Julie says. "She was disgusted."

"And she just figured out at that particular time that her car was a shithole? I mean, it didn't happen overnight," I say.

"No, it didn't. She told herself that she would clean the van out when she got home. Her husband was already home from work when she got there. He offered to help and bring the groceries in."

"Good man," I say.

"After the bags were in the kitchen, he told her that the van was a mess and she really needed to clean it. Then he sat down to watch some television," Julie says.

I know where this is going. Husband didn't offer to clean it or take it to the car wash.

"No, he didn't," Julie says. "At that point, my client said to herself, 'Fine with me, if you're not going to do it, I'm not cleaning it either,' or something along those lines."

"Sounds like basic human nature to me," I say.

"It does, right? All about control," Julie says.

"He didn't offer to clean the van, so she decided she wouldn't either," I say.

"And that got me thinking about how the minivan shows up in a lot of different ways," Julie says.

I hated that minivan.

"Don't you see? The minivan pops up all the time in relationships," Julie says. "The minivan is an example of her trying to exercise control. It really is silly. She thought the thing was a mess, but because he didn't offer to clean it, she wouldn't either. It's juvenile of course, and she is a well-functioning adult, working, married, and raising a family."

"Not exactly a rebellious or lazy teenager who doesn't feel like cleaning the car. I get it," I say. "But why doesn't she just ask him to clean the stupid thing?"

"She thinks he should just do it without her having to ask. He knows it is dirty, he should know that she wants him to clean it," Julie says.

He didn't get the memo apparently. But still, why not cut through the games part of it and just ask her husband if he would mind giving it a quick cleanup?

"If she had asked him to do it," Julie says, "then she would have given up the control. She wants it to be *his* idea. If she asks him, and he does it grudgingly, he has essentially wrested control from her."

"He did her a favor, so she owes him," I say.

"Right. And if he doesn't do it, and instead says, 'Hey, it's your car, why don't you clean it,' there again she has lost control," Julie says.

"So, what does she gain by being silent, not saying anything?" I ask.

"She can be mad, use it again, later in some other situation," Julie says. "Like she won't have sex with him, won't do his laundry, 'Those are your clothes after all, you wash them.'"

"Sounds like control is almost a commodity in relationships that can be used to manipulate the other person," I say.

"Sure is. Don't clean the minivan, no hand job for you," Julie says.

My wife smiles and asks for a towel.

I hand over the towel, and head off to bed knowing exactly where I am going first thing tomorrow: the car wash.

Bumper Cars

"You don't try to collide with pedestrians or other vehicles when driving a car. The same principle should apply in your relationship."

–Julie

Tuesdays really wipe me out. I am up at five to try to get a workout in, then drive in traffic for an hour or so to my job where I spend about eight hours in a windowless cube meeting with one client after another. If I am lucky, I get ten or fifteen minutes somewhere in there for lunch and clock out around 4:30 for another commute home, a quick dinner, and then two or three more clients at my home office. It is a grind, but the price I pay to have my long weekends.

David is already running the bath for me.

"You are so good to me," I say.

"Long day tending to various mental health deficiencies?" David asks.

I was still thinking about my last appointment. The two of them made me think of bumper cars.

"You know, like at the carnival," I say. "These people have been together for twenty or so years, married for about fifteen. Raised kids, Stuart works in the accounting department, Terry is a stay-at-home mom."

"So, what is the problem?" David asks.

"They bicker incessantly. Almost as if they hate each other," I say. "You know when you are on the bumper cars, people are aggressive and try to get in the way of the other cars?"

"Smash into them really," David says.

That's exactly what these two are doing to each other. Not physically. It's more of a "fuck you" kind of contest. And a lot of it is simple, seemingly unimportant stuff.

"Terry doesn't like that Stuart wears sneakers all the time," I say.

"So, why doesn't she take him to get some other shoes?" David asks.

"She says she did, but he won't wear them. Stuart knows she hates his beat-up old running shoes but wears them anyway," I say.

Apparently, Stuart wears those shoes all the time. Out to dinner, to the movies, friends' houses, everywhere.

"So, when you asked him about the shoes, what did he say?" David asks.

"Here is the crazy thing," I say. "He says he doesn't really like them. The new shoes that Terry got for him are fine, but not only does he enjoy irritating her, he makes sure she knows that he enjoys irritating her."

"Sounds like they could be heading my way. His joy in the relationship comes from pissing her off," David says. "And what does Terry do to retaliate?"

Terry goes into passive aggressive mode. She refuses to clean up the house; makes sure that when he comes home the place is a mess.

"Their kids' sports gear is all over the family room, the kitchen, as he puts it, looks like 'late night at the local shithole,'" I say. "Wherever that is."

"So, this guy who only wears decrepit sneakers gets wound up over his countertops not being wiped down?" David asks.

Ironically, that is exactly right. Her letting the house go is purposeful. Terry knows full well that it bothers him.

"There is a lot more to it with these two. They don't forgive each other for things that happened years ago, even if one has apologized.

No snide comment or negative act is forgotten no matter how far back or how meaningless it might have been," I say.

They are doing their best to bang into each other, get in the other's way. There can't be a healthy relationship if the two people involved continually ignore common courtesies, look to fight, find, and exploit the other's weaknesses or pet peeves.

Like I said, they are banging into each other, almost for fun. They get pleasure out of it.

"Bumper cars," I say.

David is nodding and smiling. He likes my bumper cars analogy.

"In a healthy relationship, contrary to the bumper cars, both people pay attention to the rules of the road. They drive with care, yield the right of way, proceed with caution when the light is yellow, that sort of thing," I say.

"They are not looking to get enjoyment out of crashing into the other, I get it. Bumper cars. Very creative," David says.

Maybe I can come up with something for the zipper ride or a haunted house.

Stay out of My Tub

"There might not be an 'I' in 'we' but there needs to be."

–Julie

I cannot believe that man thinks he is getting in this tub with me.

"Mind if I hop in real quick?" he asks.

He promises that he will be in and out, that I won't even notice.

He says he can't take a shower because there is no hot water left. He is probably right about that. Between me, two daughters, a son-in-law, and two grandchildren, there is often not enough hot water to go around by this time of night. It's winter, it's cold, and everyone wants a hot bath. I feel bad for David, I do.

"You could use a cold shower anyway," I say, stretching as far as I can from one end of the tub to the other.

"Funny. Seriously, it's late and I need a quick cleanup."

Let the moping begin.

"You'll come in here, splash around, crunch me to one side of the tub, and take my shampoo," I say. "Won't be two minutes before you start asking if you can wash soap on my boobs."

"They do look like they need a good soap-down though. You've had a tough day," he says.

"Nope. Not happening. Go take a shower, run under the hose outside, don't care what," I say. "You are just not getting into this tub."

It's all about space. I don't get a lot of my own space during the course of the day. This is my space, my time. And I don't want David in my space and interrupting my time.

In any relationship we all need some of our own time and our own space. I talk to my clients about it all the time. Most people need time to themselves. Even in the best of relationships.

"Like ours," David says.

Not at the moment.

"You have spent a lot of time over the years yapping at me about being on the same page, spending quality time together, parenting as a team, talking, and listening," he says. "So how exactly do you reconcile those two sides of things? We're a team on the one hand, leave me alone on the other?"

"Because it is not this hand or that hand, Mr. Lawyer. Not everything has two sides or two parts," I say.

A good relationship has a lot of parts to it. Sometimes those parts are separate, but even then, they are working together.

"So, your keeping me out of the tub somehow is a function of our working together?" David asks.

If he would just listen to me instead of staring and hovering, I could explain it.

"We take care of our kids, deal with their issues together, right?" I ask.

He nods.

"We go away for weekends, have a date night together just about every week, yes?"

"Yes," he says.

"We watch TV together after work, go to the gym and work out with each other, right?"

He nods again.

"You picking up on a theme yet?" I ask.

"You did mention the word 'together' a few times," he says.

Together is great, it is what I want and what works for us—most of the time. But another part of our enjoying our time together is our spending some time apart. For me, that means quiet, peaceful time just to sit in here, read a magazine, watch one of my home shows, or even just close my eyes and soak.

"Our being apart from each other is just as important as when we spend time together, is that what you are trying to say?" David asks.

"One is not ranked higher or more of a priority," I say. "Alone and separate time is important, that's what matters. It works both ways. You need your time, too. It's not that I don't love you."

"You just don't want me around," he says.

At this particular moment, he is entirely right.

"Why are you laughing?" I ask.

"Because I just wanted to clean up real quick," David says. "Had you let me pop in, I'd have been in and out by now and you would be basking in your alone time. Instead, you spent ten minutes giving me another lesson in Relationships 101 and your water is probably getting cold."

Lesson learned, I hope.

You've Got to Have Friends

> "There is nothing unhealthy or inappropriate about maintaining friendships and connections outside of your relationship."
>
> *–Julie*

My mom likes Bette Midler. I am just not musically inclined, but I often think of one of her songs when I am working with couples, many that think they need to spend all of their free time together, that there is no time for other relationships or friendships except for theirs. The lyric that always comes to me is "you got to have friends." Couples generally can't survive without other relationships.

"Love's not enough?" David asks.

"Nope," I say.

We need to stay connected to people outside of our marriage. I know I do. He does, too. It's a good thing for everyone. It's good for the partners in the relationship. And whatever is good for both of the people in a relationship, that is good for the relationship itself.

"I like going out with my buddies as much as the next guy, but how is that good for our relationship?" David asks.

"You have a different relationship with your guy friends than with me. My relationships with my girlfriends are different also," I say.

"But how does our maintaining friendships with other people directly connect to improving the relationship between you and me?" he asks.

"Think about what you talk about with your friends. How that differs from what you and I talk about. Things you do together also," I say.

"We don't talk about much, really. Sports, sex, and food. We spend a fair amount of time making fun of each other, but basically that's it," he says. "And what do we do? Play golf, play cards, watch sports, drink, look at women, tell stories about women. No real complexities there."

As if I didn't know what he and those morons do when they got together. He even wrote a novel about it.

I think he is exaggerating. I cannot believe that men don't ever talk amongst themselves about anything more important than who did what to which girl back in high school or college.

"Shouldn't you have real-life discussions with your friends rather than talking about the tits on some girl from high school?" I ask.

"We like tits," he says. "Seriously, though, most of the time, and I can only talk about my experiences with my friends, it really is not too much on the real-life side. There are times, particularly when one of us has something going on that is difficult to deal with, a parent dies, a kid is in trouble, business is bad, that we might talk for a few minutes about those types of things. The whole Natalie situation came up every so often, still does. But it doesn't occupy the conversation. We are not getting together to mourn our losses, get washed up in pity. We get together to have a good time."

"So, it's a few minutes of what's really going on and stuff then back to the tits?" I ask.

"Back to the tits," he confirms.

When I am with my friends, it is a lot different. We give each other support and advice. We talk about our relationships, our marriages. What are they fighting about? Financial problems. We talk about our kids. Not just the good Facebook, social media kind of stuff either. The hard things.

"In some ways, and this sounds weird, it's a measuring stick," I say.

When I say "measuring stick" I don't mean in a "me versus her" way. It's not a competition. It's a sharing of our lives, what's good, what's bad, successes and failures. We help each other.

"Having girlfriends, knowing what is going on in their lives, it's like taking a picture on your phone using the panorama setting. You can see something with a wider lens, maybe in a way you did not look at it before. Bringing that perspective, that new, fresh look, it helps when I am with you in our day-to-day life, as well as dealing with an issue or problem that we may otherwise disagree on."

"It gives you a different perspective. Hearing from someone you know, you trust, about what is going on between us," David says.

"Right. It's more of me getting a better sense of why you think what you do," I say. "It gives me the chance to talk to someone about the things that bug me about you."

"That should be a short conversation," he says.

"Months at least," I say. "Years, maybe."

It's that wider lens thing. By hearing what goes on in other people's relationships, it is easier to get centered. Listening to what is going on in the lives of other couples is a stark reminder that every relationship has its challenges.

Weekends Away

"Weekends away with friends are beneficial and healthy to a couple's relationship. But please, keep your clothes on."

—*David*

Julie still remembers the first trip away I took after we had kids.

"It was three weeks after Amanda was born. April 24 to April 26, 1989," she says.

Just as I am starting to be a little suspicious that someone who can't get a song lyric right, any song, any lyric, remembers a two-day boys' weekend thirty years or so ago . . . she fesses up.

"So, I made the dates up," she says. "It was around then, though. Not hard to remember. I had Amanda maybe three weeks before and that was after I spent three months on bed rest. Amanda is jaundiced and barely sleeping. You head off for a golf weekend. No grudges," she says.

Sounds like a grudge to me.

"Somehow you made it through and survived my forty-eight hours away," I say.

"It took us a while but we both now know that you going away was a good thing. And it's been a good thing ever since, for both of us. I go with my friends, you go with yours," she says.

"I am still having trouble getting my hands around that nude beach thing of yours, though," I say.

"When in Rome," Julie says.

I feel much better.

"When you first started going, I was not happy about it," she says. "The kids were young, and they were all needy. It was hard to do everything for two or three days on my own."

What I remember is that whenever I would come home, there was always some major hell to pay.

"You were pissed about something. Even if there was nothing wrong, you would find something to be angry with me about," I say.

"First of all, we were younger. The kids were little, and they were difficult, particularly Natalie," Julie says. "Plus, I seriously think the girls felt that since you were away, it was okay to act up."

In other words, the Sheriff was out of town.

"I do think we were a few years in before you started going with your friends," I say.

"Yeah, that's when I realized I was wrong," Julie says.

Hold the door! My wife is actually apologizing for all that bitching at me on those Sunday afternoons when I would get back?

Not so much.

"You deserved it," she says. "I was wrong not to start going myself earlier than I did."

We seem to agree that getting away from each other has been a good thing for our marriage.

"I don't think it's so much our getting away from each other," Julie says, "although sometimes that is not a bad idea. The best thing for me was not having to get anyone juice."

No one asking her for sex either, I suppose.

"I didn't say no one asked me for sex," she says. "Kidding. Yes, you're right. That was a big one, too. Still appreciate that benefit."

"You sure know how to make a guy feel good," I say.

She says I should not take it personally. I don't. Absolutely not. I definitely should not be offended when my wife says she is happy to be away so she doesn't have to have sex with me.

"When the kids were young, it was just, I don't know, nice," she says. "All I had to worry about was me. I got to relax. I was off duty."

I understand that feeling. It's the same for me.

"The other thing, to be honest with you, was that my being away made me appreciate you more," Julie says. "I could leave and I knew you had it covered; the girls would be fed and taken care of. No one would end up in the hospital," she says. "Not having to worry, that was a really nice piece. You were capable, competent. It made it easier for me to enjoy my time. I have always appreciated that."

"I never really expected that you would be surprised I could take care of the kids," I say.

"I was happy and appreciative," she says. "Didn't you feel the same way? You knew you could go away and everything would be okay?"

"I never worried about that, to be honest. I was just happy to go, be on my own," I say. "Do my own thing. Like you said."

I know a lot of guys who never go away without their wives. When I mention that I am gone two or three weekends a year, most of them look at me like I am speaking Klingon or some otherworldly language.

The truth is that we don't go to get away from each other, although that does have a certain benefit. We go because we enjoy being with our friends, doing our own thing without each other every so often.

Time away is good for people. Being a couple does not mean we have to be tied together at the stake. We can be in love, be best friends, but still be independent people, doing what we want without the other, at least for a few weekends a year.

"It's the 'me time' that I still really enjoy," Julie says. "I do what I want to do and I don't worry about whether you want to do it, too. The other aspect is just the lighter side of it. We make jokes, talk about sex, and drink wine. Just have fun. Just laugh."

And go to nude beaches.

Ruby Slippers

"There was a reason the Wicked Witch of the West wanted Dorothy to hand them over."

–Julie

If there is one thing that makes me happy, it's when a client and I talk about employing a strategy to help with a particular situation or problem and the next time I see her, she tells me that she gave it a shot. I'm even happier when it works.

"I figured there had to be something that has you grinning like me when I peek at you in the shower," David says. "What little sliver of brilliance did you impart to the lucky client?"

"She followed the Yellow Brick Road," I say.

My man is mystified.

"You know how sometimes one of us just wants to talk through a situation or problem?" I ask.

"Sure. Usually that happens when I am working, watching a game, or reading the sports page," he says. "Right then is when you decide it is time to flesh out some seemingly complicated situation with a client."

"Life is all about timing," I say.

"Or when you want to talk to me about a run-in you had with a weird dude at the grocery store," David says. "Remember the guy who you thought was staring at you while he was squeezing the vegetables?"

He is mocking me. It wasn't just the vegetables. I saw him in the frozen section, too.

"He was feeling up the frozen pizzas and waffles as I recall," David says.

The mocking continues, but there was not anything funny about it. He tried to talk to me while holding a box of waffles and all I could think of was how to finish my shopping and get the fuck out of there.

"You were still jabbering about it when we went to sleep," David says. "I had to put my earplugs in. Just nodded and said 'mm-hmm' every minute or so to make sure you thought I was listening."

"Forget the grocery store for a minute," I say. "Remember last week when I had that situation with the woman at work?"

I came home so upset. She said some things to me that sounded as if she thought I was being dishonest. A lot of what she said did not seem appropriate to me.

"They weren't appropriate," David says.

It was one of those things. I am a therapist, a social worker. I am trained to get along with people, treat people nicely, and find ways to work out differences. In this situation, a supervisor thought I lied about being sick the week before and essentially asked me for a doctor's note explaining my illness and to confirm I was telling the truth. It was good for me to have David there, knowing he cared, and that he was listening.

"You didn't laugh, cut me off, or jump in and offer advice," I say. "You let me talk, rant, whatever. Eventually I got to the problem-solving part."

Part of a good relationship is knowing what the other person needs in terms of support, help, or backup. During the conversation, I might raise a problem, and during the course of us talking, I ultimately figure it out.

"You came to the right conclusion yourself," David says.

I did, but having him there to help me along was a key to my getting there. That's what I mean by taking the Yellow Brick Road. It happens all the time in my sessions with clients.

"Just this morning, a woman who I have been seeing for years started talking to me about a problem she was having with her son," I say. "I was listening but not interrupting or cutting her off. During the course of the session, she started identifying possible solutions, things she might be able to do to solve the problem," I say.

"She could have gotten to Oz whenever she wanted. She didn't need to tussle with that wicked witch, or the flying monkeys," David says.

I told her to imagine that she was wearing Dorothy's ruby slippers. Dorothy just had to click the heels together and she would get help and support from Glinda, the good witch. Like Dorothy, my client was holding the answer the entire time.

"She just had to talk through it, click those shoes together, and go down the Yellow Brick Road a bit to find it," I say.

"You let her talk and by doing so she found the answer to a problem that she pretty much knew the entire time," David says.

That's all that being a good partner is sometimes. Not trying to solve a problem or fix something but just to sit, listen, and let the other person get to the solution on their own, using what they already have right there at their disposal.

"I get it, my pretty," David says.

The Best Chicken in the Pot
I Ever Ate

"Not everyone has a healthy, loving relationship. It doesn't
come easy. Stop and appreciate yours."

—David

Sometimes I wonder if there is a most important reason, one thing
above all others that has stood out and been more vital than anything
else in keeping us together for all this time.

We had our share of financial struggles and stresses, most brought
on by our own stupidity. We raised a child who was mind-bendingly
frustrating, has mental illness, and seemed to purposefully do whatever
she could sometimes to make life miserable in the house.

"Is there one thing you can think of, one factor that was central to
our getting through all of that?" I ask. "Aside from luck."

"Finding each other was lucky," Julie says.

I was thinking more of gratitude.

"I just don't think people are appreciative enough in terms of what
they have. I have always tried to appreciate you and me, what we have
together and in our lives. Even during the most difficult times," I say.

There are a lot of people I come in contact with that are miserable,
but they shouldn't be. A lot of time and effort is spent wishing they had
what others did.

"First world issues, I like to call them," I say.

What I mean by that is simple. We live in an area where there are a lot of people who have nothing to be jealous about, nothing to worry about. They aren't worried about real-life issues, like food, clothing, and shelter. They are terribly anxious and buried in angst over private school applications, SAT tutors, vacations to Greece, and plastic surgery.

"What do you have against plastic surgery?" Julie asks.

"Not me," I say. "Those breasts of yours were one of my all-time greatest purchases."

"Well, thank you," she says. "In fairness though, I don't think it's easy to focus on the good when someone is dealing with a lot of stress or hardships."

When we were going through the worst of times with Natalie, it was hard to stop and appreciate how lucky we were to have a family, warts and all. Constantly wrestling with emotional outbursts, dishonesty, and abuse made it easier for us to lose sight of what was good in our lives. Mental illness will do that to a family.

"It's not that we didn't love her, you know that," Julie says.

"Of course we loved her. But she sapped our energy; took everything out of us," I say.

"Absolutely. In all ways, as parents, as partners. Everything. She caused so much stress in the family, between the kids. And between us," Julie says. "We fought a lot."

We didn't have sex too much either.

"Do you remember what it was like to manage that kid's life from morning to night?" Julie asks. "Setting her alarm half an hour early, give her medicine, time to get up, back in, make sure she gets dressed, brushes her teeth. Downstairs for breakfast, whatever you gave her she didn't like. Drive her to the bus stop because I wasn't sure she would get there if left alone, and that's all before seven o'clock. Come on, by the time I got into bed there wasn't much urge to do anything other than sleep."

"I agree with you one hundred percent," Julie says. "It is so important in a relationship that both people feel gratitude, and are thankful for what they do have instead of dwelling on or wallowing over what they don't."

"Maybe everyone should get one of those rubber bracelets as a reminder," I say. "Something that says 'gratitude' or 'be thankful' or something along those lines. My grandfather was great at that."

At the end of my first year in law school, my father and grandfather drove to Chicago to pack me up and bring me home for the summer. The night before driving back, we went out for a big steak dinner at an old Chicago joint, Gene and Georgetti's. Of course, my father, my roommate and I all ordered some big fat porterhouse steaks. (Pittsburgh style, yes.) But my grandfather had high blood pressure, was watching his cholesterol, all that. He ordered a chicken in the pot.

"That's so sad," Julie says.

That's exactly what I thought at the time. After a while, our steaks get there and they are about the size of a baby bear. They gave us these four-pound steak knives meant for King Henry or someone like that and in the three of us went. We were grunting, moaning, and carving until the meat was gone. It was a carnivore's heaven.

"Sounds lovely," Julie says. "You guys are having these great steaks, and he is stuck eating some plain chicken that he could get at home. He must have been a little bit jealous. Did he say anything?"

"He said, and I will never forget, 'This is the best chicken in the pot I ever ate!'"

"Love it. There's our bracelet."

Couple's Kickstarters

1. Do you or your partner have trouble apologizing?

   _____

   _____

   _____

2. Is your relationship an "equal partnership?" Is one person in the relationship more dependent on the other? If so, is that a good thing for the two of you or does it cause conflict?

   _____

   _____

   _____

3. Do you and your partner have periods in your relationship that seem particularly happy, even "perfect?" Are there also times when you cannot stand each other?

   _____

   _____

   _____

4. Is there anything that you feel is missing in your relationship? Have you talked to your partner about it?

_____

_____

_____

5. Are there occasions when you feel your partner is not listening or paying attention to you? How do you react? Do you talk to them about it?

_____

_____

_____

6. Is there anything in your relationship or within your family that you keep to yourselves and don't talk to others about? Why?

_____

_____

_____

7. Are there things that you regularly expect of your partner? Are they reasonable? What happens when you don't feel that they have met those expectations?

_____

_____

_____

8. Do you find that your partner is too controlling in your relationship? Not controlling enough? Does control cause conflict between the two of you?

_____

_____

_____

9. How do you and your partner support or help the other when one of you is stressed or challenged in some way?

_____

_____

_____

10. Are you able to take time for yourself? Does your partner understand the importance of your doing so?

_____

_____

_____

11. Do you both maintain outside interests, relationships, and friendships? Are you both supportive of the other doing so?

_____

_____

_____

12. Do you feel appreciated in your relationship? Do you express your appreciation for your partner? How so?

_____

_____

_____

THE TAKEAWAY
On and On

The two of us were leaving an exercise class at our local gym about a year ago when one of the trainers walked up to us with a fifty-something-year-old woman in tow. She was wearing the usual gym attire; black yoga pants cropped an inch or two above her cross trainers and a tank top underneath a black track jacket. Tammy, the trainer, introduced her to us as long-time clients. "These are the Bulitts," Tammy said. "Listen to Julie so you don't need to talk to David."

"She's right, isn't she?" Julie asked in the car, already knowing the answer.

In both of our careers, stress has been a constant companion. At David's office, it may be the wife whose husband has been caught cheating and taken their savings. In Julie's, it could be a parent angry with her partner who did not do enough to keep their child from failing at school. Both of us might well be meeting with someone whose relationship has become frayed and fractured due to years of not listening or not communicating with each other.

Despite those pressures, we feel honored that people choose to share their most private, complex, and often agonizing aspects of their lives with us. One afternoon, we were out walking our dogs. Julie talked about a client, a local married woman who, after three sessions of describing an unhappy relationship with her spouse, admitted to Julie

197

that she had been having a long-time affair with a neighbor. "I am the only one she has spoken to about this," Julie said. "I feel privileged that people let me into their lives like that."

In compiling this book, we did not spend hours researching, studying, or constructing and analyzing a "love lab" as John Gottman did in his *The Seven Principles for Making Marriage Work*. Our lab is our work. Our lab is our own experience; it is late-night phone calls, emails, texts, and working with clients in our offices or coffee shops. Our lab is our home, the challenges we have faced as a couple, as lovers, as friends, and as parents. Through our conversations that have stretched over several years, our lab brings out the good, exposes the bad, and lays bare the ugly.

It is said that we learn from our mistakes, that failure is the best teacher. At the same time though, it seems to us that we should also learn from our successes and find a way to repeat and reproduce those successes in other aspects of our relationship.

The two of us may be "professionals," but we assure you that we don't have all or even most of the answers. What we do have, though, is an understanding that in a relationship, there are always questions. Questions that need to be asked, respected, carefully considered, and thought through. Most of all, they need to be talked about.

–David and *Julie*

About the Authors

Julie Bulitt, LCSW-C obtained her master's degree from the University of Maryland School of Social Work. She has served as a clinical supervisor and early childhood mental health consultant for the Montgomery County (Maryland) Mental Health Association, and an adoption therapist for the Center for Support and Education in suburban Washington, DC. For over a decade, Julie has maintained a private therapeutic practice for family, couples, and individual therapy with a focus on ADHD (Attention Deficit Hyperactivity Disorder) and Executive Functioning coaching. She is also employed by Premise Health as the in-house therapist for the Discovery Channel in Silver Spring, Maryland. A Licensed Clinical Social Worker, Julie has spent more than twenty-five years working with individuals, couples, and families.

David Bulitt, JD is a partner in the Washington, DC Metro law firm of Joseph, Greenwald & Laake, PA. For more than a decade, he has been chosen as one of the Washington area's top divorce lawyers by multiple publications and recognized as one of the "Best Lawyers in America" and a Washington, DC Metro "Super Lawyer." Praised as "the lawyer who epitomizes stability and old-fashioned common sense" by Bethesda Magazine, David has a particular interest in families with special needs children as a result of his personal experiences in his own family. A member of the Maryland, DC and several federal bars,

David focuses his practice on complex family law cases, helping his clients through complicated divorce, custody, and other contentious domestic conflicts. He has been appointed by judges to act as Best Interests Attorney for children in contested cases and, in addition, is often called upon to mediate contested domestic disputes. Drawing on his personal and professional experiences, David has also authored two published fiction novels, *Card Game* (2015) and *Because I Had To* (2017). Additionally, David has been a special guest on several local television shows and has had multiple articles published in the *Daily Record*, a regional publication read by thousands of lawyers, financial professionals, and business people throughout the Washington, DC Metropolitan area.

David and Julie Bulitt have been married for thirty-three years. They have four daughters, two of whom are biological and two adopted, three grandchildren, and two dogs. They are habitual barflies and can often be found talking to strangers at local restaurants and bars in suburban Washington, DC and Bethany Beach, Delaware.

Acknowledgments

Thanks to our parents, who have set an example for us to follow after more than 110 years of marriage between both pairs.

Thanks to our friend, Lyric Winik, whose late-night emails gave us plenty to think about and much that found its way into this book.

Thanks also to our "two other Julies." We could have not found such a wonderful publishing home without the hard work of our agent, Julie Gwinn, and the good folks at The Seymour Agency. It was a random cold call a few years back that connected us with Julie Schoerke, a Nashville publicist and our favorite cheerleader. We'll never forget Julie's note after she read our manuscript: "If I had read this ten years ago, I would still be married!"

Finally, we want to thank our children who have listened, often in embarrassment, through more than a few of the topics covered in this book. Sorry to say, girls, the embarrassment will continue.

Index

A

acceptance, 68
Acorn Shop, 3
addiction, 101–103, 109–110, 112
adoption, 66, 78–81, 110
    traits, 80–81
adult alone time, 3–4
affection, 20
Albelin, Ernest L., 76
alcohol, 31–32
A Man's Job, 126
anger, 55
apologizing, 26, 159–160
appearances, 20–22
appreciation, 185
arguments, 31, 169–170, 175–176
aspiration, 68
Assbook, 165–166
attention, 21
    paying attention to partner, 169,
        171, 176

B

The Bachelor, 5
balance in relationship, 155–195
    and boredom, 163
    dependency, 156
    highs and lows, 161–163
balance of power, 53–55

basketball, 88–89
    make it, take it, 89–90
behavioral and child therapist, 76
believing you can, 35–37
Big Four couples' problems, 44–45,
    128–129
Big Time RV, 17
blaming, 107
The Blessing of a Skinned Knee
    (Mogel), 105
Botox, 48–49
building and filling, 1–40
bumper cars, 174–176
Butt Man's European Vacation, 126

C

candy store, 3–4
cars, 63–64
Chapman, Gary, 16
chicken in a pot, 192
children, 45, 66–68, 75–118
    behavioral problems, 85–87,
        98–100, 110, 156
    behavioral problems and siblings,
        114–115
    cost of raising, 67
    illness, 96–97
    making own decisions, 92
    mental illness, 95–97

number of, 66–68
religion, 91–94
and triangulating, 77
Christianity, 92–94
Christmas tree farm, 98–99
cleaning, 6–7
  garage, 8–9
  relationship, 9–10
CNN, 67
Cocoon of the Uninformed, 57–58
Cold War, 54
communication, 25–26, 49, 155,
  157, 170. *See also* Tone
  about money, 61–62
complacency, 22
compliments, 21–23
compromises, 67–68
connection, 5–7, 25
consistency, 162
control, 172–173
conversation, 171
cooler, 28–30
Costco, 158–159
Couple's Kickstarters, 38–40, 72–74,
  116–118, 151–153, 192–195
courtesies, common, 176
CraZanity ride, 161
criticism, 28–29

D
Deliverance, 28
Diagnostic and Statistical Manual of
  Mental Disorders (DSM), 45
disability, reading, 105–106
disagreements, 157
divide and conquer, 77
divorce
  as an option, 163
  and children, 67
  impact of, 36–37
  and money, 56–58, 67

and pornography, 140
reasons for, 45
risk, 36
and sex, 119–120, 123
Dominion Hospital, 95–97
driving, learning to, 50–52
dry cleaning, 20–23

E
Einstein, Albert, 157
endometriosis, 79, 125

F
Facebook, 46, 164–166
failure, 198
Fantasyland, 123
fertility treatments. *See* Infertility
fighting, 104
first world issues, 190–191
The Flintstones, 25
Ford Thunderbird, 43–44
forgiveness, 176
foundation. *See* Building and filling
friends, 12, 180–182
  female, 181–182
  male, 180–181

G
garage, 8–9
Gene and Georgetti's, 191
Going RV, 17
golf
  bag, 53
  clubs, 25, 37
Gottman, John, 198
grandparents, 50–52
gratitude, 189, 191

H
habit, 47
hall pass, 22

Hanna-Barbera, 25
Harvard, 63–64
Hatch, Richard, 85
Hilton Head, 86–87
homelessness, 110

I
individualized education program
    (IEP), 105–106
infatuation, 161–162
infertility, 78–80, 125
    and sex, 125–126
Initial Client Interviews, 41, 162–
    163
insecurity, 167–168
Internet, 140–141

J
jealousy, 65–66
Jeep Commander, 33
Judaism, 91–93

K
key ring, 31–32

L
Letters to Our Daughters, 109–115
listening, 37, 188
The Little Engine That Could (Piper),
    35, 37
5 Love Languages (Chapman), 16
love tank, 16
lubrication, relationship, 5–7

M
manipulation, 102
mental illness, 95–99, 190
    stigma, 97
Midler, Bette, 180
minivan, 171–173
mistakes, 198

mistrust, 168
Mogel, Wendy, 105
money, 41–74
    budgeting, 47
    and children, 66
    debt diet, 41
    decisions about spending, 69–71
    and feelings, 48–49
    ignorance about, 57–59
    and jealousy, 63–65
    knowledge about finances, 56–59
    overspending, 43–44, 60–62
    savings, 60–61, 68
    tit for tat, 54

N
Natalie (child), 76, 80, 86–87, 91,
    95, 97–103, 105, 109–115, 181,
    184, 190
newspaper, 46–49

O
O'Jays, 41
Orgasm Alley, 126
orgasms, 19
oxygen masks, 14–16

P
painting, 19
parenting, 14–15, 75–118
    and addiction, 101–103, 109,
        112
    and behavioral problems, 103
    cause and effect, 88
    and enabling, 107
    and failure, 106
    make it, take it, 90
    mental illness, 95–97, 190
    and perfection, 105, 107
    and religion, 91–94
    rescuing, 108

on the same page, 76–77
turn taking, 82–84
passive aggression, 175
Pass the Trash, 82–83
perfection in a relationship, 7
physical contact, 131–133
Piper, Watty, 35, 37
poker, 82
ponytail test, 51
pornography, 126–127
    causing relationship problems,
        141
    and cheating, 139
    and relationship, 138
    and unrealistic expectations, 141
proving things to others, 64
psychiatric hospital, 95–97

R
Red Rover, 89
relationship
    blanket, 5
    parts of, 178
    success, 162
religion, 91–94
Repo Man, 58
repression, 169
responsibilities, sharing, 52
rewards, 76
roof, 11–13
RV, 17–19

S
Seinfeld, 166
self-care, 9, 12
self-sufficiency, 50–52
*The Seven Principles for Making
    Marriage Work* (Gottman), 198
sex, 5, 7, 45, 55, 79, 119–153, 167
    bad sex, 142–144
    blowjobs, 142–143

boredom, 135
communication about, 146–147
creating conflict, 146
and differing needs, 128–130
and disrespect, 146
drive, 128–129, 148
dry humping, 143
and fantasies, 135–136
frequency of, 122–124, 134–135
hand jobs, 148–150
and happiness, 120
hitch in the giddyup, 135
importance of, 131
and infertility, 125–126
and love, 140–141
and porn, 125–127, 138–141
pressure to have, 128–129, 146
problems having, 143
and relationship, 140
and respect, 129
as a responsibility, 145–147, 149
and routines, 134–135
threesomes, 135–136
The Shining, 87
shoes, 53–54
silence, 24–26
    silent treatment, 24, 26
    when to be silent, 31–34
social media, 164–166
softball, 89
Sonny the golden retriever, 47
Soviet Union, 54
space, 178
support, 18–19, 187
Survivor, 85
swimming pool, 71

T
talking things through, 187–188
time
    being busy, 12

management, 13
to yourself, 178–179
time-out, 25
tit for tat, 54–55
togetherness, 178–179
tone, 27–30
touch. *See* Physical contact
triangulation, 76–77
tub, 177–179
tumult, 162

U
Understanding the Divorce Cycle
(Wolfinger), 36
United States, 54
Urban, Keith, 22–23

W
War of the Roses, 54
Washington Post, 46, 164
weekends away, 183–185
White Coat Syndrome, 80
Wilderness programs, 101–102
windshield, 99
The Wizard of Oz, 155
Wolfinger, Nicholas, 36

Y
Yellow Brick Road, 186–187
Yeti, 28, 30
YouTube, 105

CPSIA information can be obtained
at www.ICGtesting.com
Printed in the USA
LVHW112217031122
732354LV00017B/220

9 781510 746121